GENERATION *EX*

GENERATION EX

TALES FROM THE
SECOND WIVES CLUB

KAREN KARBO

BLOOMSBURY

Published by Bloomsbury, New York and London
Distributed to the trade by St. Martin's Press

Library of Congress Cataloguing-in-Publication Data

Karbo, Karen
Generation Ex : tales from the second wives club / Karen Karbo. –
1st US ed.
p.cm
ISBN 1-58234-126-5
1. Remarriage. 2. Divorced people – Conduct of life. 3. Wives –
Psychology. I. Title.

HQ1018.K37 2000
306.84–DC21
00-049848

I'm Henry VIII, I Am
Words and Music by Fred Murray and R.P. Weston
© 1965 (Renewed 1993) FRANCIS, DAY and HUNTER LTD.
All Rights for the U.S. and Canada Controlled and Administered by
GLENWOOD MUSIC CORP.
All Rights Reserved International Copyright Secured Used by Permission

First U.S. Edition
10 9 8 7 6 5 4 3 2 1

Typeset by Palimpsest Book Production Limited,
Polmont, Stirlingshire, Scotland
Printed in the United States of America by
R. R. Donnelley & Sons Company, Harrisonburg, Virginia

For My UPS Man

'In the sex war, thoughtlessness is the weapon of the male, vindictiveness the weapon of the female. Both are reciprocally generated, but a woman's desire for revenge outlasts all other emotions.'

Cyril Connolly

'Any marriage, happy or unhappy, is infinitely more interesting and significant than a romance, however passionate.'

W.H. Auden

'Forty-seven per cent of people who are divorced or separated personally know someone who's going to hell. Some even claim to have slept with them.'

Break-Up Girl

CONTENTS

Acknowledgments

Many people have put up with me during the writing of this book. Thanks go to Kathy Budas, Bill and Joyce Loftis, Ken Loftis, Megan McMorran, Whitney Otto, Danna Schaeffer, Dan Weiss, and Lisa Zeidner for their eternal patience and good humor. Steven Allred, Dan Berne, Greg Cliburn, Dig McIntyre, Hillary Jordan, Tom Spanbauer, and Mike Taylor were all more than generous with their thoughts, opinions, and war stories.

Dan Newman deserves a special medal.

Kim Witherspoon has supported this project from the beginning. I thank her for her fortitude. The congeniality award goes to David Forrer, also of Witherspoon Associates.

I am grateful for the insight, appreciation, and wit of Ann Patty.

I am beholden to the incomparable Karen Rinaldi for being both my champion and task mistress, also to

Panio Gianopoulos, who suggested the title and did more hand-holding than his job description demands. Thanks to Susan Burns, Sandee Yuen, and Claire McKinney, also of Bloomsbury, and Jean Lynch, my copy editor. Finally, I am indebted to all the exes I interviewed who have suffered through divorce, and lived to laugh about it. In the end, what else can you do.

The Underpants Episode

The idea for this book presented itself about five years ago when my then-boyfriend's ex-wife broke into his house in the middle of the day and cut the crotch out of my underpants with a pair of cuticle scissors. I should say I wasn't wearing the underpants at the time.

Matthew and I were in line at the movie theater, hoping to hide out for a few hours in the air-conditioning (Portland was in the middle of its annual August heat wave) when Claudia, Matthew's ex-wife, called his cell phone.

'You better get home right away and explain whose *crap* this is or I'm taking a crowbar to your truck. And I'll tell you something else, *she's* going to have to answer to *me*.' I could hear her voice through the phone. All I could think of was Darth Vader.

The 'crap' in question was my clothes slung around

Matthew's bedroom, my laptop and manila folders stuffed with work in a pile by the bed, my optimistic assortment of face creams strewn around the bathroom sink. I was only staying with Matthew for a week while the wood floors in my house were refinished, but it probably looked as if I was all moved in.

Matthew dragged me out of line before Claudia even had the chance to hang up on him. The whites of Matthew's blue eyes function like a mood ring; when he gets distressed they go pale pink. He also chews his upper lip, leaving it perpetually chapped.

He sped back to his house as if it were a real emergency, eyes bloodshot, munching his top lip until it bled, courting a triple-digit speeding ticket. I stared down at my thighs. They were trembling with fear. I must say I found this interesting: until that moment I'd thought 'trembling with fear' was a literary conceit.

I knew three things about Claudia: she'd once gotten so mad she kicked in the kitchen cabinets with her cowboy boots; another time she got even madder and put her head through the wall; she also loved animals, especially pigs and sheep.

I come from a family of staunch Episcopalians who like to curl up with a good book in a straight-backed chair. We show our anger by refusing to get angry. I worried Claudia might come after me with the crowbar, but the prospect of watching her stage a full-scale tantrum, complete with weeping, cussing, and clawing at Matthew's sleeves, was also terrifying. As we drove to his house I remember thinking: These two people have been divorced for four years – twice as long as they were married. Why is this kind of high drama still going on?

For I was also divorced, and my relationship with my ex-spouse was nothing like this. We were, and are, Monty Python-skit polite – '*After you.*' '*No, after you.*' '*After you, I insist!*' We conduct ourselves as if we are the tetchy diplomats of warring Middle Eastern nations. We are *politesse* personified. Our divorce was so amicable, we shared the same attorney. When we went downtown to meet with him, we'd each try to leap out of the car first, competing for the pleasure of feeding the meter.

I didn't understand this business with Claudia. I assumed that because two people were divorced they'd forfeited their rights to badger their former partners. I'd led a sheltered life. I thought only married people did things like threaten to bash up their spouse's truck with a crowbar. If you didn't want to participate in this kind of event anymore you forfeited the game, undocked the spaceship – apply whatever severing metaphor you think appropriate. In a word, you got divorced.

We pulled up to Matthew's house, a gray bungalow surrounded by rhododendrons that bloomed Las Vegas pink in the spring. His gleaming silver truck was parked at the curb. Claudia's dented green Geo was parked in front of the truck. The truck was untouched, which was sinister instead of reassuring. Now I thought maybe it would explode. Matthew unbuckled his seat belt, fed the shoulder strap into its proper spot, chewed his lip. I could tell he was trying to figure out how to handle this. He taught English at a public high school where no child can be sent to the principal's office unless she's broken a desk or blackened someone's eye, which caused Matthew to be a man who buys time in a crisis. I, on the other hand, have the habit of hurling myself into the fray. The fire might kill me, but it's better than the gut-twisting apprehension of the frying pan.

'Stay by me,' said Matthew.

'This is ridiculous,' I said. 'Just go ask her what she thinks she's doing.'

As we got out of the car, Claudia suddenly appeared in the doorway, steered out of the house by a small woman with dirty-blond hair parted in the middle, tucked behind her ears, and a tall guy with a narrow chest wearing a backwards baseball cap. They were thin and unremarkable compared to Claudia, who reminded me of some large oceanic creature attended by spindly pilot fish. They held Claudia by her upper arms, as if she might collapse or escape.

Claudia avoided our eyes, meditated on the tops of her large white running shoes. Matthew said later that one of the interesting wrinkles in Claudia's personality is that unlike many nutcases she lives in a state of constant worry that people will think she's a nutcase. (I knew he didn't really think Claudia was crazy, and only said this as a show of solidarity, but I appreciated it anyway). I looked hard at the part in her hair, hoping to start it on fire.

Matthew and I had been dating (or whatever it is that exes do; 'dating' sounds so collegiate) for six months, but I hadn't yet met Claudia. One always likes to see the competition, and the ex-wife is always competition, even if it's only in the category of memories and a shared past, a more significant category than one ever suspects.

She was pie-faced, with perfect teeth, a double chin, and the kind of spectacular auburn curls that are featured in hair-coloring ads. She had the kind of big, round body – hands like mittens, plump shoulders, forearms, calves – that made nineteenth-century portrait painters swoon. This latter part made up for the terrific hair, I was not unhappy to note.

Her auburn curls did not catch fire, nor did she look up. Her pilot fish guided her to her car. Weirdly, no one said anything, as if her being escorted out of Matthew's house in the middle of the day by her buddies–cum–parole officers were a normal occurrence.

Inside, it was difficult to tell whether the house had been trashed or not. Matthew shared the rent with a pair of bicycle delivery guys still in college, and their refined sense of decor prevailed. The dining room table was invisible beneath mounds of junk mail, sun-bleached circulars, empty plastic liter bottles of Diet Pepsi, paper plates smeared with red sauce and some petrified strings of pasta, a stack of white tube socks, the tops of each pair folded over on itself. The living room had a big TV, a treadmill, and a dusty leather sofa whose arms had been scratched to shreds by past cats.

Matthew had been in the Air Force for a time just after high school, and his room reflected this. I don't mean to suggest you could bounce a quarter off his bed, but the bed was made, the laundry put away in a small chest that sat in the closet. There was nothing but the bed and a wooden cabinet with glass doors, a huge piece meant for the dining room, the one piece of furniture from their marriage for which Claudia apparently had no use.

The first thing I saw when I walked into his room were my jeans, T-shirts, and underpants strewn about the bed, my blue duffel bag turned inside out and kicked into a corner. On the floor was a snapshot of me, snipped neatly into dime-sized bits. Missing from the window ledge over the bed were Matthew's address book and an extra set of keys normally stored in a green milk glass bowl.

What did people do before film was invented? How did they interpret that thump in the gut that makes modern victims of bizarre circumstance think 'this is like something out of a movie.' Or, if it's particularly cheesy, a TV movie-of-the-week.

I contemplated the empty green bowl, imagined Claudia somewhere on the freeway, plotting her next move, his house keys in her hands, her promising that she'll come back and . . .

'Know what?' I said. 'I'm not sleeping here tonight.'

I marched into the bathroom to collect my toothbrush. That's when I found my underpants crumpled up on top of the toilet tank, the crotch snipped out with the small bending points of the scissors Matthew used to trim the ends of his moustache. All the lotions and potions from my overnight case had been dumped into the sink. There were deep half-moon gouges made by acrylic fingernails in the tubes of hair shampoo and toothpaste – no human nails could have made those slices. Almond-scented body gel had been squirted all over the inside of my cosmetics case. She'd broken off a tube of lipstick, pulled the mascara wand out of its dark blue cylinder and bent it in half. My deodorant had been twisted all the way up, the lid then smashed back on. Such well-considered destruction for someone so presumably full of uncontrollable rage.

The phone was ringing, had been ringing. I heard Matthew answer it in the other room. As I was trying to figure out what to do with the mess, Matthew came into the bathroom and wrapped his arms around my waist. He was a backstroke star in college; his arms are long and strong. Behind me, through the receiver, I could hear Claudia shouting. 'You and that slut will pay for this. I am going to make it my goal to ruin your life, and hers. Do you understand?'

Over the next several months I revisited this moment too often, long after Claudia apologized and Matthew forgave her. Whenever we argued, I would bring up the Underpants Episode, and snarl at Matthew 'Who cares how sorry she was. It's easy to be sorry after the fact. Why didn't you just tell her you were calling the police? Why didn't you say "Here in the civilized world it's called, 'breaking and entering'. It's called 'vandalism'. Do *you* understand?"'

He had only one reason to simply let it go. The reason all exes with children know, the best reason of all. No matter what she did, Claudia was still the mother of their daughter, six-year-old Erica.

Some time later, I was in a salon getting my hair cut. Tattooed Gina, who also happened to be an ordained minister and had on several occasions the gratifying experience of doing the bride's hair, then marrying her, has lots of stories about exes. Hairstylists always do. Gina herself has an ex-husband who periodically shows up in the middle of the night and weeds her front lawn in an effort to prove he's changed his slackerish ways. I told Gina about the Underpants Episode. I was proud of the story by then, felt it was exotic, rare, as delectable in the telling as a Third World travel misadventure. The day

Claudia cut up my underpants was like the day I got mugged in Caracas, or survived the emergency landing of a 727 on the Micronesian island nation of Palau. Gina listened, combed through my wet hair, stuck it up in huge silver clips, and cut. I could tell she wasn't surprised.

A large woman in clam diggers eavesdropped from the pedicure chair. 'Excuse my interrupting. You're not married to Ron Gerber, are you?'

I said no, I wasn't married, and I didn't know any Ron Gerber.

'That's *his* ex-wife's thing.' She said it as if it was a comedy act, or a talent the ex routinely performed at a beauty pageant.

'Anytime Ron'd get a girlfriend, the ex-wife would go over to his house and cut up her clothes. The girlfriend's clothes, I mean. I don't know what type of scissors she used. It may have been those scissors that come in the middle of those wood blocks of knives. Know the ones I mean? Anyway, it got so Ron would say, "Don't leave any clothes at my house if you want to see them again." Some of his girlfriends thought it was him having an intimacy problem, and one confronted him on it. "Suit yourself," he said. Then one day the ex-wife was dropping off the kid or picking up the kid or one of those things, and saw a pair of the girlfriend's running shorts, those silky kind, and ripped 'em right in half, just as if she was making dust rags or something. Ron is actually the guy who painted our house. If you ever need a house painter he's pretty reasonable. And he shows up on time.'

'He should have called the cops,' I said. The same suggestion I'd made to Matthew. But by then I'd learned there's no such thing as breaking and entering for ex-spouses. Legally there is, obviously, but not emotionally. The ex broke in and entered long ago, has already been there and gone. What's the point of calling the police?

'What was he going to do?' said the woman in the pedicure chair. 'They had a kid together.'

Exactly.

Before this, the Underpants Episode had struck me as aberrant behavior, the kind of scenario cooked up for those daytime TV talk shows, where it's been said that most of the head cases are really low-rent actors. I tried to compare it to *Fatal Attraction*, but the algebra wasn't right: I wasn't married to Matthew, but neither was Claudia. Nobody was married, nor were any of us cheating. The simple explanation was that Claudia was insane.

A simpler explanation was that Claudia was an ex-wife who hadn't been able to get on with her life, as all exes are advised to do, as if we are loiterers with nothing better to do than hang around the old marriage, waiting to set a trash can on fire or throw a rock through the window. Which some of us are.

I began comparing notes with people I knew who'd

been divorced. What I thought I was doing was gathering evidence that Claudia was not insane, thus clearing Matthew from having had the bad judgment to marry, and father a child with, a lunatic. Along the way I also discovered that a lot of people, an entire generation of exes, were having many of the same experiences.

Friends, acquaintances, neighbors, colleagues, fellow writers and teachers, the mothers and fathers at my daughter's preschool: all it took was a casual question – 'You used to be married, didn't you?' – to encourage them to talk. I heard from the baby-faced Estonian who owns the neighborhood espresso place, the mechanic with the gold front tooth who services my car, my regular checker at the neighborhood grocery. Every ex had his or her own set of bizarre, heartbreaking, blackly comic stories of revenge, depression, and the new complexities of falling in love and marrying *again*.

There are more of us out there than one might imagine. Between 1966 and 1976 divorce rates in America doubled, so that a little less than half of all marriages now end in divorce. Although currently rates seem to be dropping a bit, they've remained steady for almost thirty years. This means that everyone under fifty or so knows exes, is the child of exes, or is an ex him- or herself.

Abigail Trafford's book *Crazy Time: Surviving Divorce and Building a New Life* was recommended to me by the FedEx man. It's one of a handful of self-help books that succeed in demystifying the extreme emotions surrounding divorce (read: convinces you it's normal to feel homicidal, suicidal, incredibly young, lucky, and sexy, then dull, fat-assed, and dumb as dirt, all in an afternoon), but is a little weak on the 'building a new life' part.

Yes, after the shock, grief, depression, loneliness, and hard work of getting back on your feet, there is a light at the end of the tunnel. What no one tells you is that the light illuminates an awful lot of people, especially if you have children. There you are, crawling from the wreckage of your divorce, decree in hand. You've stood up, dusted yourself off, and who is left standing there with you? Your brand-new ex (you didn't confuse the death of your marriage with actual death, did you?); your new lover or spouse; your ex's new lover or spouse; your new lover or spouse's ex; the ex of your ex's new lover or spouse; and maybe a bunch of kids of various parentages. It's the huge shock of divorce: you're not married to your spouse anymore, but it doesn't mean you're out of relationship with him, either. As an oft-married matron once said to me, 'Honey, marriage is for ever, but divorce is for life.'

There is a section in *Harry Potter and the Sorcerer's Stone* where Harry arrives at King's Cross station to catch the train to Hogwarts, the wizardry school where most of the book takes place. The train departs from platform 9¾.

To the eyes of the average Muggle, as non-wizards are known, there is nothing between platforms 9 and 10 but a barrier separating them. Only when Harry meets another family sending their wizard sons off to Hogwarts, does he learn that to get to platform 9¾ he must run straight at the barrier. 'All you have to do is walk straight at the barrier . . . don't stop and don't be scared you'll crash into it, that's very important. Best to do it at a bit of a run if you're nervous,' he's advised by the mother of his classmate. Just before smacking into the wall, he's whisked into an invisible new world, a parallel universe where wizards rule and Harry himself is as famous as Prince William; a magic place that occasionally makes itself known to the real world in the form of owls who deliver the mail, and visiting wizards who disguise themselves as alley cats. Because this is essentially a story for children, life on the other side of the barrier is quite wonderful. Happy endings abound.

Exville is not unlike Hogwarts, invisible to the eye of both the never and happily married, but as real as pork chops for those of us who have taken the D-train, departing from a platform only other exes know about. It's a place not unlike cyberspace, or bacteria, for that matter: always there, but invisible. It's a place where we worry about stepping on our ex's toes, then go right ahead and hurl the crockery anyway; where we obsess about whether and how we should acknowledge the birthday of our ex, not simply because he is our child's other parent, but because it might be the best thing to do. (Common sense would suggest that you ignore the birthday, but is that modeling birthday-ignoring behavior for your children, and thus contributing to the decline in civility everyone complains about these days?) And what about your anniversary? What do you do with *that?* It's a place where children – whose resilience and forgiveness we divorced parents spend our lives praying for – tend to live in two houses, with two beds, two night-lights, two sets of broken Happy Meal toys left in strategic places to step on in the dark, two sets of special books and stuffed animals.

It's a byzantine place. Once a couple of exes have found new partners, there are more considerations than ever. How do you cope with your new love's hateful ex, the mother or father of his or her beloved child? How does your new partner cope with the fact that your own ex has failed to move on, and still pines over you (or shows up unannounced to weed the lawn)?

It's a place rich in complicated attachments, a nineteenth-century Russian novel updated and come to life. In many ways, the so-called binuclear family, a phrase coined by Constance R. Arhons in *The Good Divorce*, has replaced the extended family as the contemporary family model. My mother grew up in the 1940s in Ipsilanti, Michigan. Her father died when she was young, and her mother, my grandmother, ran a boardinghouse. On the bottom floor of the three-story brick house lived my grandmother, my mother and her two older sisters, the oldest sister's husband and their newborn, and Aunt Ellen, the official family spinster. Until the day she died my mother was never sure whose aunt Ellen really was.

My family looks like this: a wife/mother/ex-wife/step-mother (me); a husband/father/ex-husband/stepfather (my husband); my ex-husband, who lives across town and with whom I share joint custody of Katherine, our daughter; my husband's ex-wife and her new husband (who live out of state); my daughter's grandparents, who live two miles away; my stepchild's grandparents, who live in a neighboring suburb. Hillary Clinton, hear this: All the children are treated as grandchildren by all the grandparents. My ex-mother-in-law often asks after my husband. My ex-husband has had my daughter's stepsibling over for a sleepover. You get the point. Call it what you will, the family of this generation of exes is the same old mismatched group of people with conflicting personalities and desires the world has ever known. My Aunt Dot, now eighty-seven, once said, 'In a room of a hundred people, pick the ten people you like least, and they will all turn out to be members of your family.'

Like the wizard world of Harry Potter, this ex world makes itself known in the real world, but you must look carefully. Recently my husband (here's another wrinkle:

I'm tempted to write 'my current husband', but that presumes that one day he will be yet another ex-husband. Having multiple spouses creates the same dilemma known to fifth-graders learning how to outline. If you have a 1, you've got to have a 2), my ex-husband, and I went to parent conferences at our daughter's school. Conferences are held in the cafeteria, where each teacher has his or her own card table set between a pair of partitions. The school is pre-K through eighth grade, so there were about a dozen card tables, six in a row on each side of the room. Around each table were enough folding chairs for the teacher plus four parents, not two. As we sat down, my ex, my husband, and I noticed that, true to the statistics, at almost half the tables sat a configuration of parents that included stepparents.

You know you're through the 'crazy time' Trafford writes about so well when the craziness has become more like a chronic condition (unfortunately, colitis is the one that comes to mind) than the full-blown case it was three weeks after the separation. Now you only lose your mind around Christmas, or when the ex decides to get married, or moves to an ashram, or advises your only child to consider the military. You can tell it has passed when you feel all right enough to pass all those books on to friends who need them more. But your life isn't easy. You're still an ex. You still need a book for after the aftermath of the divorce. I'd like to think it's this one.

This book is not an apologia for divorce, although I expect it will be taken as one. About 20 million American adults have been divorced and one in three American children will spend some time living in a stepfamily. And it's not just an American phenomenon. In Canada, 30 per cent of marriages end in divorce. In France, it's one in three. In Britain, which has the highest divorce rate in the fifteen-nation European Union, it's two in five. In Russia, two thirds of all marriages end in divorce. In Catholic Chile, divorce is illegal, which means the unhappily married rely on annulments; there are about 6,000 a year, and countless separations. In the last two decades in China the number of couples seeking divorce has tripled. For better or for worse, it's time we treated divorce like the established social institution it is.

Professional pro-marriage crusaders tend to assume that anyone who writes about how one might make the best of life after divorce is an enemy of marriage, failing to see that almost everyone who divorces eventually remarries, which is either a testimony to: a) the validity and desirability of matrimony or b) the stunning stupidity of the human race.

I don't presume to know how wretched life can be for ex-wives and ex-husbands who are mired in extreme poverty. Or for people like Ivana Trump, whose divorce settlement from Donald Trump included $14 million in cash, a penthouse in Manhattan, a house in Connecticut, and $650,000 a year in maintenance (the new janitorial-sounding term for alimony) and child support, a woman who says, 'The only time you don't need a prenuptial is if he has no children . . . and he's got a bad cough and a walker.' Yoick, yoick, yoick.

None of the people I talked to had a prenuptial, and all of them have to work for a living. I've changed all their names and identifying characteristics to preserve their privacy.

Unlike Harry Potter, who leaves Hogwarts (unhappily, it must be said) and returns to his Muggle aunt and uncle through platform 9¾, we exes can never leave the place where we find ourselves after we've divorced. It's a parallel universe, but there's no crossing over. This is particularly true for divorced parents, who are always bound to each other through their children. We imagine, when we divorce, that we are escaping the disappointing relationship, the cruel spouse, the doomed marriage. What we are actually doing is creating a new affiliation defined by what it was, but isn't any longer. It's the Law of Thermodynamics as applied to human relationships. In the same way that energy can be neither created nor destroyed, so too a dissolved marriage remains forever a dissolved marriage. It never becomes a marriage that never was; the children are never unborn; the heart never unbreaks.

1

The Mae West Dinner Party

My ex still lives in the house we bought together before we were married, a small yellow bungalow where he has lost the war against junk mail, a war I'd spent fighting every day of our marriage. Long ago I read a magazine article about getting organized, and took the organizational expert's advice to heart: Allow mail to flow through your hands only once. It either goes in the wastebasket, or you deal with it now. During my reign as my ex's wife, junk mail never made it as far as the kitchen table. Now, when I drop our daughter off there, or pick her up, I can't help but notice that the junk mail has taken over every flat surface: the dining room table; the console of the vintage stereo; the small table our daughter used to draw at when she was a toddler. I'm suddenly bowled over with a weird sorrow inappropriate to the occasion. It's only free downloads from AOL, still in their plastic envelopes, catalogs, and credit card solicitations, nothing poignant to remind me of our six-year marriage. Yet as I watch him bend down to write a check for his share of our daughter's school tuition, I stare longingly at the top of his head. He has a Jackson Browne head of semisweet chocolate-brown hair, now graying, straight and shiny, which our daughter has had the luck to inherit. For a minute I wish I could take it all back; my part in the divorce, and his part too. This wave of regret and nostalgia for his great hair is followed by a wave of resentment. I'm divorced too, and *my* house isn't buried in paper. And while we're at it, why am I the one who collects his portion of the tuition, then writes the check for the full amount to the school? Why isn't joint custody synonymous with joint bookkeeping? Then that feeling is followed by plain guilt. For being petty, and for being divorced from a decent human being.

By all rights I should now move into how and why my marriage to my ex failed. That would be the logical narrative progression. I would tell you how difficult my ex was, how living with him became impossible. I would reveal all without compunction because he is after all, my ex. I was wounded. He was wounded. All is fair in falling out of love and the subsequent cold war. I might try for an insouciant tone, work the subtext and innuendo, but his faults would all be there. I would present my case for leaving him – statistically, women tend to be the leavers (75 per cent of all marriages are ended by the wife) while men prefer to make a marriage so unbearable that a woman has no choice but to leave; in any case, a man almost never leaves a marriage unless he's got someone to leave it for. I would demonstrate with the skill of a prosecuting attorney why the divorce was inevitable. I would do this because to simply say 'Things just didn't work out' sounds too much like a statement issued by the White House.

I won't do this, however. It violates one of the few ironclad rules we Generation-Exers feel obliged to try and uphold (it should be noted that we often fail): Never criticize your child's other parent in front of your child. I could make the self-serving argument that this narrative was written for adults and has nothing in common with, say, standing in the middle of the street and shrieking at your ex that he's a heartless son of a bitch, while your child sits on the front porch waiting to be taken to soccer practice, but I don't buy it. Eight-year-old Katherine already reads the newspaper, and spends an unnerving amount of time snooping around my desk. Saying anything about her beloved Daddio would get back to her, somehow, and hurt her in a way I can't imagine, and the fact it was an act of self-expression won't matter to her. Katherine's also decided she wants to be a judge when she grows up, and being her mother, I'm sure she would practice her sentences on me.

The essayist and undertaker Thomas Lynch found this out the hard way. In *Bodies in Motion and at Rest* he writes about the time his daughter heard him read his gloriously nasty and brilliant poem 'For the Ex-Wife on the Occasion of Her Birthday.' A sneering seventy-line litany of things he claimed *not* to wish for her (loose stools or blood in her urine, among them), it was a huge crowd pleaser.

Once, with my darling daughter in earshot, I was coaxed into reading it to a group of writers in a summer workshop in northern Michigan. It had earned a certain celebrity by now. To my everlasting shame, I never thought how much hearing it would hurt her. And by the time I saw the pain and confusion on her face, I was too far into it to turn around. Or I was having too good a time being the center of attention. Later, I tried to tell her that the poem was really not *about* her mother, but *about* my anger, and that as a poet, I had artistic rights and license in the matter, that I was entitled to my feelings and their free expression. To her credit she did not believe me.

Like a cheap insurance policy, however, my vow of discretion regarding my own failed marriage does not cover other people's. I'm not that well-behaved. Most exes love to dish about each other, and don't mind if you repeat what they have to say. A lot of exes are happy to have someone else spread the bad word about the one who done them wrong. 'It's more therapeutic than therapy,' says a hospice care nurse I know who's been divorced twice. 'A therapist is obligated to hear you out, but will never give you the satisfaction of nodding her head and saying, "That slime dog!"'

I learned the degree to which ex-wives love to talk, and talk to anyone, at a divorced-women-only dinner party co-hosted by my roommate and best friend, Kiki. I also realized then that Kiki and I weren't the only women we knew with peculiar households, but part of a whole slew of exes bumbling around, trying to figure things out.

Kiki and I were roommates at film school in Los Angeles in the early 1980s. She is my oldest friend, and my onetime role model for what I thought a personal life should be: rife with intrigue, a French farce minus the farce, one man coming in the front door while the other is scooting out the back. She called her boyfriends 'lovers', and us, 'women' (rescuing me from a lifetime of calling us 'gals,' the word my sorority sisters had used).

The Kate and Allie House was Kiki's name for the house we shared, the same house she had lived in when she'd been married to Mort. She named it after the 1980s TV show with Jane Curtin and Susan St. James, who were divorced moms with kids. When we were bored Kiki and

I liked to revive an old-married-couple-style argument about who was Susan St. James (pretty, sexy) and who was Jane Curtin (funny best friend of pretty, sexy Susan St. James).

The Kate and Allie house looks like a kid's drawing, with two rectangular window eyes on the second floor, a steep roof brow, and a porch that sags in the middle like a smiling mouth. Two huge oaks were planted in the tiny front yard by someone who failed to read the fine print; the trees dwarf the house and in the fall their orange leaves collect in three-foot-high drifts.

The first half of the week Kiki and I had our kids, Phillip, then eight, and Katherine, who'd turned three the month I moved in. They slept in bunk beds in a small room we painted a demented aqua. Sunday through Wednesday we were moms, fretting over the differences between a PG and PG-13 video, trying to figure out ways to liven up the macaroni and cheese, and yelling at Philly and Katherine to '*Stop bickering or we'll pull off your arms and beat you with the bloody stumps.*'

We cracked ourselves up. If we'd stomped around and said stuff like this when we were still married, we would have thought we were turning into our mothers. Now, since we were living in the Kate and Allie House, our parenting styles were showy and boisterous, ironic.

When Kiki cooked, Philly and Katherine would eat

in front of the TV on the glass coffee table. On the nights when I cooked, I made us all eat at the dining room table, which Kiki thought was ridiculously middle class, but I insisted. My theory is that most of what we call 'civilization' are table manners, and that our most meaningful contribution to society and culture is teaching our children that it's inappropriate to wipe their mouths with their collars.

During the second half of the week, it was our old roommate lifestyle. We bought red wine by the case and in the evening sat at the same wooden kitchen table we'd had in our apartment in L.A. nearly twenty years earlier. The kitchen was small, high-ceilinged, covered with thick, inexpert coats of eggnog-colored paint. Kiki still had the same black-and-white portable TV that had sat on the table years before, a TV on which we had watched thousands of installments of the *Today* show, and the news about John Lennon's murder. On the wall was the same plug-in wall clock that for unknown reasons, sometimes ran backwards, perfectly.

'Have you noticed that men are much better fathers after they're divorced? One more reason why divorce is truly so much better for women than for men,' said Kiki one night, waiting for her cheese soufflé to cook. She stood with her freckled arm reaching out through the back door, a Marlboro between her fingers. (The Kate and Allie House had a serious no-smoking policy.) Kiki is lanky, with pale skin, chin-length reddish-blond hair. In a past life she could have been a flapper.

'Your ex has to become a man, instead of enjoying his former role in the marriage as a tax-paying adolescent. Mort now has to be responsible for Philly when he's there. When we were married, Mort would agree to watch Philly. Translated, that meant he would watch a basketball game on TV and allow Philly to be in the same room with him. If Philly got hungry, or started emptying the bookcases and eating pages of a book, which is something he did, Mort would yell for me to come get him. Some child care, huh?'

On another night she proclaimed, 'The only way to have a good ex relationship is not to take any money. Ever. I get no alimony and no child support, and Mort and I get along just fine. Except when he does something so stupid I want to kill him, like putting an ad in the paper for Valentine's Day. Did you see this ad? It says, "Kiki! Drop everything and have dinner with your men!" Meaning him and Phillip. Normally you'd think, "Ah, that's sweet." But it's so, so inveigling. It's manipulative. And then I have to disappoint Philly, because of course he's in on the joke. Divorce isn't the end of the bullshit, it's just the end of the marriage. All it means is that you stop fighting in the kitchen and start fighting over the phone. Most of the time, you haven't been sleeping together anyway.'

Kiki dubbed the divorced-women-only dinner the Mae West Dinner Party. She's worked for a long time in marketing and public relations, and finds comfort in high concepts, and in naming things that don't normally have names.

The Mae West Dinner Party was for divorced women who, like Mae West, felt that 'Marriage is an institution and I'm not ready for an institution!' I thought it would be curmudgeonly to point out that as divorced women – and some of the guests had two marriages behind them – we had all at one time been enthusiastic supporters of the institution, and if the statistics were right, 80 per cent of us would move into the institution again.

Married women have secrets. A better use of the veil at the wedding ceremony would be to have it lowered *after* the exchange of vows, so when the bride walks back down the aisle, she's covered up and no one can see the expression on her face. Now that she is on the arm of the groom, she will become more inscrutable to the outside world.

Next to the lengths to which she has gone to make herself look great in a swimsuit, the biggest secret a woman has is the nature of her marriage. These aren't necessarily dastardly secrets. Sometimes they're silly. Sometimes it's what she puts up with, the flaws of her mate that the rest of the world doesn't know, her husband's dumb tics, his eccentricities. Sometimes they're big secrets that, if revealed, might color the way the world views the wife; sometimes they're secrets of no real consequence that would merely embarrass her husband. But while one is married to the husband, while one is still in love with him, one doesn't want the world to know that he obsesses about his nose hair, or is deathly afraid of the water bugs that show up once in a while in the kitchen.

An ex-wife, on the other hand, has no obligation to keep the secrets of the marriage. Just the fact of the divorce is letting out a big secret: The marriage didn't work. She is free to tell all. And she will.

Forget all those self-help books, seminars, and industrial-strength wedding vows people are taking these days in Louisiana. If you don't want your husband to leave, tell him you'll tell everyone you know everything you know about him. And tell him you know more about him than he thinks you do. That'll make him think twice.

The party was held at a tiny lavender shake-shingled bungalow in a part of town with used-mattress stores, food co-ops with the original psychedelic signs, and a Starbucks tucked in to show that while funky, the neighborhood was still desirable. Esther, the hostess, is fifty and has been married and divorced twice. She's a dancer (modern, not exotic) and has such flair that she can hang a T-shirt on the wall and call it art. Esther smokes and doesn't care. She still wears Levi's 501s, size 30-32. I don't think I know anyone older than twenty-two whose waist number is smaller than their length number.

If there is such a creature, she is sure to be an ex. At the time of the Mae West Dinner Party, I was as thin as I'd been at twelve. Which, for the record, did not make me happier, but made me feel as if I was perched on a ledge somewhere, waiting for the fire rescue squad to show up. I was thin because I was tense. As was everyone else at the party.

Bruce Springsteen was on the CD player, moaning about being on fire, just as he was in the mid-1980s, when all of us were involved with the 'perfect' guys who turned out to be imperfect. We drank Spanish red wine and gobbled young Brie cheese, not the collapsed, odoriferous type that signals French cheese, but the Costco version that looks like something Katherine played with in her toy kitchen.

The only woman I knew there was my roommate Kiki; the others were graphic artists, managers of nonprofit organizations, florists, a framer (pictures, not houses), an attorney, the tiny blue-jeaned dancer, Esther. We were between thirty and fifty, had attractive red rinses in our hair, enjoyed pedicures and facials now and then, had seen the capitals of Europe during the low season, flossed. We knew our astrological signs and more about our signs' personalities than we'd ever admit. Most of us had an IRA, or something like one. We wore different medium-priced perfumes, the kind advertised in upscale women's magazines. Despite our divorces we were, I'll use the word, 'together'.

A woman in a white T-shirt and black blazer reached across my lap to get to the plastic Brie and asked, 'Your husband dump you for someone else?' Leo raises funds for a nonprofit organization, which requires her to wear a suit each day and have a high tolerance for ornery rich people, so her abruptness surprised me.

'No,' I said. Feeling party-pooperish for failing to elaborate.

'I left Bernie too. We hadn't had sex for seven years. Can you believe it? Do I look like someone who has not had sex for seven years? He always had some excuse, like they say women always do. One day I went to do the laundry and all the hand towels were missing. I thought I was losing my mind. I knew socks could get eaten by the washing machine, but weren't hand towels too big? So where were they?'

I waited. She waited. I thought this was a rhetorical question.

'In the dish towel drawer by mistake?' I said finally.

'At the back of his closet, stiff with cum.' She steered a cracker heaped with cheese into her mouth. This was a woman whose lipstick never rubbed off, a well-spoken woman who also volunteered for one of those get-the-vote-out organizations, phoning people right before an election to make sure they were registered. She was upstanding.

But . . . '*stiff with cum*'? The phrase was like an invisible automotive airbag that inflated and filled up the entire room. I thought, *Eeeow, too much information*. Does anyone ever use the word 'square' anymore? Because that's what I am, square.

From across the living room a woman named Betsy yelled, 'Leo, I've always wondered about that. What'd you do?'

'I got the car and the finches,' said Leo, flipping her hair over her shoulder.

'No, with the towels. Did you put them in the laundry hamper? Did you leave them there?'

'She should have seen if she could have somehow used them for artificial insemination,' said someone named Suze, whose husband had come out of the closet, but still wanted to live with her while he dated men.

'I wanted kids,' Leo explained to me. 'My ex claimed to want kids, but then he never wanted to have sex. Well, sex with me, anyway. Clearly he didn't mind having sex with himself. Whenever I'd tell him I was ovulating – I even invested in one of those special thermometers – he suddenly wouldn't feel like it. His excuse right before bedtime was that he had to check his e-mail. Then he'd stay on the computer until I fell asleep. One day I figured out his password and checked all of this famous e-mail. It was all "How to Erase Bad Credit" junk mail. Not even any triple-X stuff. Nothing.'

Betsy, a district attorney who raises Corgis, said it could be worse. There was a guy in her office who had been so sure his wife (now ex-wife) was having an affair, he'd pulled strings at the crime lab to have a pair of her underpants tested for the presence of foreign semen.

'The test came out negative, which enraged him so much he confronted her anyway.'

'What happened?' I asked.

'What do you *think*? She was livid. They broke up. They got back together. But she just couldn't get the underpants-testing business out of her head. It's so . . . medical, or something. It's like that gynecologist whose wife filed for divorce, and he found out there was someone else, and then during her hysterectomy he sewed her vagina shut.'

'What are you talking about? That's hardly the same thing,' said a woman whose name I didn't know. She had a long face, with straight glossy black hair, a thin bony nose, and upon closer inspection, no eyelashes. She reminded me of someone famous whose face I couldn't put a name to. Then I remembered: Rafiki, the baboon from *The Lion King*.

'She was cheating on him and she *let* him do her hysterectomy!' said Leo. 'She deserved what she got. When I left Bernie I wouldn't have a glass of wine with him until the papers were signed. Hell, I'd never have a glass of wine with him.'

'What, were you afraid he'd get you drunk and then not want to have sex with you again?' said Rafiki. This was a dumb joke, but Rafiki laughed at it anyway. She had had a few drinks before the dinner party began. Later, I would learn that Rafiki was having a hard time adjusting. All those nights alone with the remote and a good book weren't quite what they were cracked up to be, especially when this could be a preview of the next thirty years.

I said, 'Wait a minute, can we back up a minute here? What happened then?'

'She filed criminal charges and that's the last I heard,' said Betsy.

This wasn't what I'd meant. Let's say she recovered from the hysterectomy, life got back to normal, then one day she was tussling on the sofa with her new beloved and . . . I really couldn't imagine this at all. I was suddenly reminded of the trouble I always had getting the straw into the too-tiny hole on the top of those juice boxes. Was it like *that*? And then, when she realized what had happened . . . how would you realize what had happened? You'd bend over and look up yourself, or use a mirror and then you'd go, 'oh, wow, someone sewed my vagina shut.' This was simply too unbelievable. It ranked right up there with the story I heard about the man in France who was so angry at his ex-wife that he killed her with a wedge of Parmesan cheese. I had to think about that one awhile too. I didn't mentally rejoin the party until we all were sitting perched on the edge of our chairs with plates full of vegetarian lasagna and fancy-blend bag salad tossed with balsamic vinaigrette dressing teetering on our laps.

Kiki sat on the floor at the Salvation Army coffee table – glass top, scarred legs, a bargain at twenty dollars — eating the cheese from the top of her lasagna with her fingers and bemoaning a current problem with Mort.

'What am I supposed to do,' Kiki said. A statement, not a question, because there is nothing to do. With exes, there almost never is. Mort, a CPA and poet, has written and self-published a book of poetry about Kiki called *My Ex-Wife Looks Like Ginger Rogers*.

'He can't just do that, can he? Expose me that way? I don't even look like Ginger Rogers. She was fat.'

There was a lot of hilarious ranting about the foibles of the ex-husbands at the Mae West Dinner Party. Their mean streaks and fits of sonic snoring, their universal impulse to colonize the bathroom and stink it up. What made them cry (modern women all suppose they want men to feel free to cry, then we're mildly disgusted when they do). Their general lack of interest in the marriage until it caved. Their universal inability to pay their child support on time (not true, as it turns out, but so what). All these men we'd lost sleep and weight over, we'd sobbed over. Villains all.

One of the things ex-wives routinely complain about is how their ex-husbands never talk. Legions of ex-wives report that when still married to their ex-husbands, they 'warned them' that the marriage was disintegrating, that they were unhappy, that it was no longer working, that they felt alone in the marriage, that they'd slept with the pool guy (just kidding; that one usually does get the conversational ball rolling), that perhaps together they should seek counseling, and their then-husbands could barely look away from the ball game or the computer screen.

The best chance I had at finding a man to represent the more measured – and, I hoped, more profound – male point of view was to interrogate Spud, who I've known since tenth grade. After two marriages, which had produced one child each, he'd landed in Oakland, California, where he wrote screenplays and an entertainment column for a dot-com content site.

Together we'd been the copy editors for the yearbook senior year. We'd had such a good time paying no attention to what we were supposed to be doing that we let slip an outstanding typo: over the spread that pictured our staff slaving away to produce a memorable, award-winning tome ran this headline in thirty-six-point type: LET'S HERE IT FOR THE YEARBOOK STAFF. This gaffe, coupled with the fact that we both became writers, united us in irony forever.

Spud is the ultimate on-line guy, a devotee of e-mail long before the movie *You've Got Mail* and even, I think, before AOL came up with the cute postbox icon and the disembodied 'You've got mail' voice.

He asked me to e-mail him my questions, so I did:

1) What were the circumstances surrounding your divorce?

2) How would you describe your relationship with your ex?

3) On a scale of one to ten, with ten being full disclosure, how honest do you feel you can be with your ex.

4) Have you ever used your intimate knowledge of your ex against her?

5) How does your ex exert control?

6) Did it take longer for you to decide to get married or divorced?

7) Divorce ends marital conflict: True or False?

8) Are you the 'good guy' or the 'bad guy' in your ex-marriage?

9) What revenge fantasies have you had against your ex?

10) Has your ex ever been abusive? If so, how?

11) Describe yourself as an ex.

12) Are you remarried? Does your spouse have an ex-husband?

This was Spud's response:

<<Have you ever watched your dog take a dump in the backyard? What's the first thing he does after he straightens up? Runs a couple feet away from the pile, then kind of struts around like it wasn't him. He wants to get away from that stinky mess ASAP, and guys feel the same way about a marriage that didn't work out. Doesn't matter who did what. Doesn't matter if he left or she left or he cheated or she cheated. Does. Not. Matter. I hope you didn't spend a lot of time thinking up these stupid questions because no guys will ever answer them. *Ever.* And don't think it's just something guys don't talk to women about, but sit around drinking beer and talking to each other about. Guys may talk about old girlfriends or wives or what have you as a topic but Jesus, never specific. And the topic only gets discussed in very general terms, VERY GENERAL TERMS, if they're all in a row somewhere – at a bar or a ball game – and then it's '*Women – alimony – Jesus – what are you gonna do – pass the Beer Nuts.*' And this isn't because they're emotionally fucked-up, like women think, but because, hey, if I answer all these questions about Eleanor and Char [Spud's exes] it makes me look pretty stupid, having married the bitches in the first place. Ex-wives are always bitches, I hate to tell you. Even if, like with Eleanor and me, I cheated

on her. I cheated on her and she got upset, which makes her the bitch. If my official position was that she's not a bitch, then why did I divorce her? Again, I look stupid. Looking stupid and looking like a failure are two things guys avoid at all costs, and I gotta tell you, it's more important than the feelings of the ex, even if she's in the right. Like both of mine were, technically. But I will answer one question. Number 7 is False. And change your interviewing approach, Karbs. Jesus.>>

2

A Personal History of Exes

One thing about being an ex of a certain age is the lack of exes in one's immediate family. We were eleven women at the Mae West Dinner Party, with fourteen failed marriages between us, and none of us came from what used to be called a broken home. More unusual still, three of us had no divorces in our extended families.

We had few ex role models growing up (indeed, it could be argued that 'ex' and 'role model' are mutually exclusive terms; the only modeling an ex provides is, *Don't be one*). This may explain our ongoing sense of confusion. Life as an ex is not simply one long rope climb; it's also a matter of weaving the rope as you climb it. There are no customs and traditions to either follow or rebel against, no ex-spouse wisdom handed down through the ages, no ex-spouse credo, no handy old ex-spouse truisms. No ex-spousal equivalent of 'He who laughs last laughs best.' (The closest thing is, 'The less said, the better.') There are a few old ex-wives' tales, but most are cheeky aphorisms by famous repeat offenders like Zsa Zsa Gabor ('Getting divorced just because you don't love a man is almost as silly as getting married because you do'), and still don't address how one might live his or her life after the dust of divorce settles.

Our married parents are no real help. Daria is a friend of Matthew's, a high school French teacher originally from Ohio, with the long limbs of a track star and a charming overbite more attractive than anything an orthodontist could have come up with. Daria took the Goldilocks approach to matrimony. Thomas was her college sweetheart. (This formerly romantic term, now synonymous with marital doom, implies not love at first sight but low self-esteem. Instead of raving through the four-year parent-supported party called college, you clung to the first guy who handed you a paper cup full of rum punch at your first dorm party. Then look what happened.) A stockbroker and former rugby player who liked to race Jet Skis and throw elaborate costume parties on Halloween, Thomas left Daria for an *older* woman, another broker, while she was out of town at a conference of high school language teachers. If Thomas was a big guy in all ways, Daria's second husband, Moon, was a little guy, a five-foot-six-inch classical oboe player who spoke barely above a whisper and who, says Daria, could sleep all night in the same position, making it look as if the bed had never been slept in. Moon specialized in Baroque oboe, and made so little money that some years he didn't even have to file an income tax return. Daria left Moon for Randy, a middle-of-the-road-guy, neither big nor little, who holds the office record for never having called in sick. She has one child with Thomas, and one with Randy, but none with Moon.

'My mom's been married to my dad for forty-four years – not years filled with joy and happiness, I might add – and she doesn't approve of any of this. She thinks I'm warped or something. She never says that, of course. She always throws up her hands and says, "I'm staying out of it!" even if it's just a question like, "Do you think Maggie's too young to take horseback riding lessons?" Mom never liked Thomas, thought he was phony, but when he left me it was like I'd done something. She's of the generation where men are like geese – you've got to run straight at them waving your arms and screaming to get them to move away. If you don't nag, you keep the bathtub free of hair, and you show up with some food around dinnertime, no husband will ever leave you. So it was my fault, and it was certainly my fault when I left Moon. The other thing she says is "I just want you to be happy!" But it's like a desperate threat. Like the way you'd say to a mugger, "Here's my wallet, just take it, take it!"

'My personal feeling is that the worse your parents'

marriage was, the more resentful your mom feels for having hung in there with a lout, or a nice, stable, but essentially bland-o guy, or whoever your father is, and the less she wants to know anything about your life as a divorced person. She sucked it up; why shouldn't you?'

My own parents' marriage, or what I saw of it, was tranquil. It was a simple fact, more like the weather than a relationship. I was surprised to learn at an embarrassingly advanced age that people considered a marriage to be a living, breathing thing, and as difficult to keep alive as an iguana in Iowa.

I grew up in Whittier, a conservative suburb of Los Angeles, where my mother was a homemaker (the word she insisted on rather than 'housewife', which sounded a bit too Chaucerian for her), and the treasurer of Las Damas, a women's club affiliated with the Rotary. She stayed away from the PTA, because she thought everything that went on at school was my business. She was a devotee of the thank-you note (she trained me never to come straight out and say, 'Thank you for the beautiful pair of socks,' but to use the more informative, flattering, 'I love my new socks. My feet have never looked better') and the kind of meals that always involve a lavish amount of simmering, like beef stroganoff. For her, divorce was not a question of morals, but one of taste. It was something We Didn't Do, in the same way we didn't put bottles of salad dressing on the table, or wear the same clothes two days in a row. We tossed the salad in the kitchen and served it in a nice teak salad bowl with matching serving spoons (preferably matching the bowl, but definitely matching each other). Clothes worn once went in the laundry, even if they weren't actually dirty. Thank-you notes were sent within a week of receiving a present. I was taught to call it 'present', not 'gift'.

Divorce was tacky, unless you were Ava Gardner, and then it was exciting, an accoutrement of the movie-star life, like limousines and shooting on location. Passionate outbursts by movie stars were a by-product of the creative temperament; normal people getting divorced was not a question of alleviating misery, but a sign of bad manners.

My parents' marriage was the opposite of turbulent. They were a man and a woman who slept in one big bed, but otherwise didn't spend much time together, which seemed fine with them, since besides me and their mutual memories, they didn't seem to have much in common.

My father was an industrial designer who chose his words as if a conversation were a simple machine that worked only with the parts it needed to run. My father lived in the garage when he wasn't at work designing sporting goods equipment or irrigation systems or the early packaging for McDonald's hamburgers. In the garage, he rebuilt English sports cars, which he never drove.

When one was finished, he'd sell it to the first taker and use the proceeds to buy another one.

My mother liked parties and the stories of the people she met at the A&P. She was a fabulous card player. Every year she asked my father to take her to Las Vegas, then wouldn't let him sit beside her at the craps table because he embarrassed her with his lack of *joie de vivre* (my mother may not have allowed me to call a present a gift, but she was the first person I ever knew who dropped a foreign phrase into a conversation to impress someone).

In the evening, before dinner, she made Old Fashioneds, which she served my father outside by the pool on a large hammered-silver serving platter she won in a bet. When I was ixteen, fifteen years before I would even consider the notion of marriage, she died. An astrocytoma in the left frontal lobe, a malignant tumor of the astrocytes, cells in the brain that are shaped like stars.

At the turn of the millennium, our marriages and remarriages bear almost no resemblance to these single-paycheck, cocktail-hour unions. Once considered sexist and monotonous, these staid marriages are emblems of an easier time. What seemed too dull and constricting a mere fifteen years ago now looks luxurious, like those huge gas-guzzling cars with all that chrome and the tuck-and-roll seats. If you don't believe me, poll some exes who've been through a divorce or two. Suddenly their parents' solid-beige marriage looks as if it might have had possibilities after all. The problem is, you have to be divorced to realize this.

There's another conundrum. Why did those of us who grew up in the kind of two-parent families that we, as well as many hand-wringing child development experts, now sometimes wish we had, wind up divorced? If those intact families were such a superior construct, if sticking it out was hands-down the best idea, why do the children of sticking-it-out become exes?

Although divorce is considered to be largely a twentieth-century phenomenon, anthropologist Helen Fisher, author of *Anatomy of Love: A Natural History of Mating, Marriage, and Why We Stray*, claims that falling out of love, and thus divorcing, is part of our chemical nature. Fisher made headlines in the 1990s when she published findings indicating that humans are hardwired for serial monogamy. She studied the United Nations surveys of divorce statistics and discovered that it's not uncommon for young couples still in their prime parenting years to divorce early in their marriages, remarry, and produce more offspring with a second spouse. This 'Four-Year Itch' (it is a title given by Fisher) has to do with adrenaline or endorphins, or maybe all those horny-making handbag ads Christian Dior has been running lately in fashion magazines. In any case, if we're chemically programmed to couple, uncouple, and recouple, there's no reason to suppose Lucy, whose four-million-year-old *Australopithecus afarensis* remains were found in Ethiopia in 1974, wasn't an early hominid Zsa Zsa with her own set of prehistoric witticisms. This study presumes there have been exes forever, not just since the Industrial Revolution, or the women's movement, or the invention of the Pill.

And yet, the history of exes is a shadow history. There are studies of divorce, but none of the average life of ex-spouses throughout the ages. There is no book entitled *The Everyday Life of Ex-Husbands from the Roman Empire to the Present*, no children's series with titles like *See Inside the House of a Single Mother During the French Revolution*. One presumes this is because men, historically the writers of history, don't wanna talk about it, as my friend Spud pointed out, and anyway, until recently women were viewed as chattel, so whatever their lives were like after they were divorced was of little interest.

What we talk about when we talk about the history of exes, is perceived history. If you didn't grow up with exes in your own house, any history of people marrying, then making each other miserable and splitting up, is what you cobbled together for yourself.

The first ex in my life was Henry VIII, who I learned about in third grade. One day I was driving somewhere with my mom and one of my favorite songs came on the radio:

I'm 'enry the Eighth I am/'enry the Eighth I am I am/I got married to the widow next door/she's been married seven times before/and every one was an 'enry/she wouldn't take a Willie or a Sam/I'm her eighth old man I'm 'enry/'enry the Eighth I am.

I knew all the words and sang along.

My mom said, 'This song is based on a real person, you know. He founded our church.'

I had no idea who she meant. Herman of Herman's Hermits?

'The real Henry the Eighth had only six wives. He divorced them or chopped off their heads.'

Divorced his wives and *chopped off their heads*? I didn't hear the 'or' in there, and thought the beheading was part of the divorce proceedings. This could be why I didn't know any divorced people, except my mom's friend Mrs Gaspin. How'd she escape? Did King Henry cut off his wives' heads himself? Was it like the opposite of putting the ring on the bride's finger?

I had a brand-new set of World Book Encyclopedias and I looked up Henry VIII when we got home. I've been studying him ever since.

If it wasn't for Henry Tudor's marital troubles there wouldn't be any Church of England, which was founded on Henry's dastardly, egomaniacal impulses but fully established by his commonsensical daughter, Elizabeth I, who wondered (preceding the ever-quotable Rodney King by four centuries) whether we couldn't all simply get along, whether it wasn't enough that we all believed in God? The thing about Anglicans is that we're fully aware of our ignominious beginnings, which keeps us for the most part humble, and therefore unlikely to launch a holy war or an Inquisition.

That said, horrible Henry retains for me immense appeal. Mostly because he makes the rest of the world's exes look good by comparison. Whenever I wonder how so many people – good people, smart people, well-traveled people, people therapized to within an inch of their lives – wind up in such complicated, ill-fated relationships, I revel in the fact that despite King Henry's majestic genes and royal blood, his wealth, beauty, privilege and power, he couldn't steer clear of exville either.

Henry was the JFK of the Middle Ages, the pre-Elizabethan Sexiest Man Alive. There had never been a more charismatic king in British history. While Henry was still a teenager he was betrothed to his older brother's widow, Catherine of Aragon, the plump, golden-haired daughter of Queen Isabella and King Ferdinand of Spain, six years his senior. Eventually Catherine and Henry were married, and for some twenty years the good times rolled. They were happy.

As in any marriage, there were problems. At the end of the Middle Ages forty was not thirty, as they say it is now, but sixty. Henry was still a dapper thirty-five when Catherine was nearing menopause, and despite the fact she had borne him a daughter, Mary, and a son who lived a scant six months, Henry still did not have the male heir he needed. (We won't go into the fact that it was his daughter who wound up being one of England's greatest monarchs.)

And why didn't he have the heir he needed? Not because childbirth was a dicey proposition in the sixteenth century, not because any man has a 50/50 chance of not having a son, but because God was angry with him and had refused to bless his marriage. It took a little digging by Henry's religious advisers, but eventually it was decided that by marrying his brother's widow, Henry had violated the Degrees of Affinity.

Loosely defined, the Degrees of Affinity spelled out which familial connections were too close for marriage, according to the Book of Leviticus in the Old Testament. You could marry your fifth cousin, but not your first. Henry followed this line of thinking then readjusted it to meet his needs; it was quite obvious that God was withholding an heir because he had violated the Degrees by marrying Catherine, his brother's widow.

As Karen Lindsey points out in *Divorced, Beheaded, Survived: A Feminist Reinterpretation of the Wives of Henry*

VIII, the Book of Deuteronomy contradicts this, saying that in fact a man *should* marry his brother's widow in order to ensure the continuation of the line, but no matter. All Henry needed was a plausible excuse. Heirs, schmeirs; the truth was this: Henry had fallen in love with a younger woman – the same old story – the dark-haired femme fatale Anne Boleyn, who refused to sleep with King Henry because, well, he was married.

Here's where the kind of information that has gotten popularized in Trivial Pursuit veers from the truth. Henry did not invent divorce. Henry did not want a divorce. Divorce as we know it wasn't sanctioned in England until the mid-nineteenth century, and even then it could be decreed only by an act of Parliament. Henry was a confirmed Roman Catholic. He thought Protestants vulgar, not to mention heretical.

The king applied to the Pope to have his marriage to Catherine of Aragon annuled, that hair-splitting definition of dissolution that allows a married couple to pretend they're not getting an actual divorce. For seven long years there was no word from the Pope, and for almost that long, Anne the Temptress, the Great Whore, the home wrecker, refused to become Henry's mistress.

There were several reasons for the papal delay. At the time, Pope Clement VII was the prisoner of Charles V, Emperor of the Holy Roman Empire and not incidentally Catherine's nephew. The Pope, while holy, wasn't stupid; to rule against his captor's aunt would be asking for worse treatment than he was already enjoying. The Pope also thought this whole business was sort of ludicrous. Then you had your ongoing skirmishes between European nations, the annual summer infestation of London with the bubonic plague, the diversions of the Italian Renaissance. In short, manipulating Church dogma to accommodate the King of England's mid-life crisis was not on the top of Clement's to-do list.

Finally, fed up with the ongoing papal dithering, Henry moved his court to the country without telling his wife. He instructed a messenger to tell Queen Catherine that he had left her, and that she should be gone before he got back. It was the end of the marriage; Queen Catherine was now The Ex. She refused to budge.

This is my favorite part. You'd think being the king of England, with his hundreds of courtiers, advisers, and scholars, with the greatest minds of the western world at work on the problem of how to get rid of one wife and replace her with another, Henry would have planned a little better. But no! The fact that the first wife wouldn't relinquish her hold on what was still rightly hers – if not Henry, himself, then the queenship – and the soon-to-be-second wife was saying, 'She goes or I go', made King Henry behave like the usual out-of-his-mind ex.

Enjoy this timeline:

July 14, 1531	Henry leaves Catherine
January 25, 1533	Henry marries Anne Boleyn in secret, while still technically married to Catherine
May 23, 1533	Archbishop of Canterbury declares the marriage of Anne and Henry lawful and valid
September 7, 1533	Birth of Elizabeth I to Anne
March 23, 1534	Pope Clement VII declares the marriage of Catherine and Henry lawful and valid
March 24, 1534	Uh-oh

For a time, there were two queens. After the Pope's ruling, there was no choice but for the king to claim that the Pope's power over English affairs was no longer absolute; thus the Church of England was born, with the king becoming the Defender of the Faith. The theological mess was left to the Archbishop of Canterbury to figure out. I can't remember who it was at the time, but he was later executed, as was anyone who didn't enthusiastically support Anne, the new royal consort.

Catherine refused to accept the turn of events, refused

to acknowledge she was no longer the queen of England. There were scenes. There was the medieval equivalent of screaming on the front lawn. Catherine had been placed in a country palace in Easthampstead with her household, where she developed an irritating habit of falling on her knees and declaring herself the king's true wife whenever an emissary of the king showed up with some more bad news. As punishment for her refusal to release her hold on Henry, Catherine and her household were continuously moved to smaller and danker and shabbier palaces, farther and farther from London.

Once, when Anne and Henry were going to visit the court in France, Anne got it in her head that since it was only a matter of time until she would be made the true and only queen (all the conservative advisers in Henry's court who refused to acknowledge her as anything other than 'a common stewed whore' had already died or been put to death), she should be given the queen's jewels to wear. Henry had to send someone out for them, but Catherine refused to give them up. As punishment, she was stripped of most of her servants.

'I would rather be torn to pieces than admit I am not the king's wife,' Catherine would say to anyone who would listen. Anne would get wind of this and order Henry to send his ex to a still-more-unpleasant house even farther from London.

Then Anne wanted Catherine and her daughter, Mary,

put to death for treason for their continued refusal to acknowledge her as the new and rightful queen. Nag, nag, nag. Henry ignored Anne. Anne continued to harp. Henry started to gain weight. He was no longer the JFK of the Middle Ages. He incurred a nasty wound while hunting that festered for the rest of his life, refusing to heal. It smelled. Soon Henry was forty-five, and still, no heir to the throne. He was unhappy.

Henry had discovered that Anne was high-strung, jealous, and opinionated. The same qualities he found provocative in a fiancée were a pain in a wife. After waiting so long to make her his queen, she turned out to be unbearable. One evening Anne caught King Henry with his new love, Jane Seymour (not to be confused with Dr Quinn, Medicine Woman), on his knee. She flew into a jealous fit, and that night miscarried a child who looked to be male.

'Anne's chief concern was that Henry would divorce her, believing this was the worst he could do. But the truth was that Henry did not want any more protracted legal proceedings to end yet another marriage,' writes Alison Weir in *The Six Wives of Henry VIII*.

Thomas Cromwell, earl of Essex, struck upon an idea that would relieve Henry from having to suffer another ex-wife. Anne was a world-class flirt. The same flirting that had bewitched Henry could easily be made to seem not part of the harmless realm of courtly manners, but the prosecutorial world of treasonous adultery. Conveniently, Cromwell was able to amass enough evidence (never substantiated) to convince Henry that his wife had had adulterous relations with five men, including her own brother. Anne was promptly dispatched to the Tower of London.

Anne Boleyn was beheaded on May 19, 1536. In honor of the fact that she had once been queen, her head was buried along with her body, instead of stuck on a pole in the public square.

The only other ex I knew as a child was the afore-mentioned Mrs Gaspin, my mother's token divorced friend, or divorcée, as they were called in the 1960s. 'Divorcée' is a peculiar word. The double 'e' at the end, the *accent aigu* on the penultimate 'e', should all work to give it a cosmopolitan flair, to evoke images of svelte, weeping heiresses in Hermès deserted by their globe-trotting husbands and forced to take up residence at the Hotel de Crillon, but instead it manages to bring to mind desperate women who smoke too much and put too much emphasis on the beauty of their feet.

Mrs Gaspin was both of these. She was dramatic. She was the only grown-up I knew who cried in public. (Or cried at all, for that matter. Like a taste for bubblegum ice cream and chocolate licorice, I always thought people outgrew their tear ducts.)

Mom and I are on the way to the laundro. I'm about thirteen. Mom drives a huge car, the Cream Dream, a 1970 Ford Galaxy 500. It's a convertible, but Mom never puts down the top because then her hairdo will get messed up.

I know it's summer, because in the summer, during vacation, Mom makes me go to the laundro with her once a week. There is no weather other than hotter-than-the-hinges-of-hell, as my mom calls it, every day without a cloud, never less than ninety-three degrees. Mom says learning to fold towels in thirds is part of my education, as is taming into submission the unruly, puckering corners of fitted sheets. She believes she's preparing me for life with a man who will expect his towels folded properly, a well-bred man with a good job that will allow me the freedom to focus on folding, but all she's doing is showing me how excruciatingly dull grown-up life can be, how being a wife is the ultimate dead-end job.

I wear ugly clothes to the laundro, because the good clothes are all going to be washed. The main ugly outfit this particular summer is a brown-and-white nubby pullover with a mock turtleneck that zips up, and a pair of beige corduroy cut-offs I've been able to wear for a full five months, a triumph. I'm still growing. I should have stopped by now, but I persist. I've been known to explode out of clothes before we can even get the price tags off. Sleeves shrink, armholes threaten to cut off circulation, sassy miniskirts become dress-code-violating, crotch-baring micro-minis in a matter of days. My mother takes me to the doctor every few months to see how she can stunt my growth. I am a weed, according to her. Behind my father's back she sneaks me coffee, cigarettes. Better to have bad breath and stained fingers than no date to the dance.

Even though I am already 5'9", I weigh only about 120 pounds. Still, Mom claims my corduroy shorts make my butt look as big as a breadbox. I don't know what a breadbox is, exactly, because we keep our bread in a drawer. On another, separate occasion Mom has also told me that I should conduct myself like Marilyn Monroe. She read in an article that Marilyn Monroe said no matter what she was doing – even if she was sitting alone in her apartment reading a book – she behaved as if someone was going to leap out and take her picture. I don't know how I can do both: go out in public with my breadbox butt and be photogenic at the same time. I hug the door on the passenger side of the Cream Dream, my knees propped up on the dashboard, the window rolled down. Mom never drives more than thirty miles an hour. She is afraid of driving, but she does it. We take surface streets. We never go on Whittier Boulevard, because it has stoplights.

I poke my pointy brown elbow out the window, my elbow that is always dirty, according to Mom, no matter how hard I scrub. The washcloth is no good, so I try a square of pumice – holey and gray, like some kind of petrified cheese – that she's given me to get the barnacles off my heels. I'm pretty sure barnacles grow in tidepools and on the backs of whales, but here they are on my feet. I'm impossible. The pumice square was Mom's present for getting my period. 'Time to smooth off the rough edges,' she said.

In the car, driving, Mom lets me listen to KHJ, because she considers herself a cool mom. A fun mom. At the music store in the shopping center where I take my flute lessons they give away stickers that say 'KHJ Rules'. Every week I look to see if they've put the Rules out, but they never do. I go for years like this, picking up the stickers on the counter near the register, looking to see if by chance KHJ has put out the Rules yet.

I haul the laundry baskets from the trunk while my mom sits inside the laundro, in the orange plastic chairs connected by a metal bar that runs under the seats, counts out her quarters, and lights a cigarette. I go over to the machine on the wall and buy tiny boxes of Tide, and Downy for the rinse. It's the hottest part of the day, and inside the laundro is hotter than outside, where the flat noon light is absorbed into the wide, black asphalt streets. My mother likes this time of day, because the laundro is usually empty. I put the quarter in the machine and feel a drop of sweat roll down my side, inside my mock turtleneck.

My mom is sorting, the cigarette stuck to her lip. Whites, colors, dark colors, sheets. Even though the sheets are also white – no colors, ever – they go in alone. Suddenly, someone rushes in and cries out my mother's name. It's Mrs Gaspin.

Mrs Gaspin is the prettiest of all my mom's friends. In my mind, she's still a person and not a mom, even though she has children. This, I see now, was an important distinction. Her divorce and subsequent life of making do made her seem as protean as any teenager. She is the only one who, as my mom put it, kept her figure, as if your figure is something that can get loose and will need to be collected at the dog pound, or forgotten about completely.

The divorced Mrs Gaspin also has smooth hands. She wears belts. Sometimes she has pimples, just like I do. My mother says the pimples are from eating at McDonald's, something that divorced women do instead of being at home cooking a proper meal. I think of all my mother's complicated recipes that can take the whole day to cook. My secret is this: I'd rather be Mrs Gaspin than my mother.

The divorced Mrs Gaspin also wears mascara and eyeliner, which is now running down her face, because she is crying. In her capri pants and flats like Laura Petrie wore on *The Dick Van Dyke Show*, she is crying. In the laundro. Sobbing. Her face is red like a sunburn.

'That bastard,' she says, unwrinkling a shredded tissue. Now she is swearing. In front of me. A child.

I stand there with the little boxes of detergent and softener and stare. Everything in me perks up, like one of the dumber mammals in the middle of a forest. I am aware of all the room I'm taking up. I tower over the divorced Mrs Gaspin, who also wears a gold anklet. 'Go do something,' Mom hisses in my direction.

What is there to do? It's the laundro. I'm already doing what I'm supposed to do.

'He said, "Give me another chance." Do I have any choice? I love him. I give him a chance – one more, one more, always one more – and then he comes home from the track and I smell her on him!'

Mom gives me a quarter to go next door to the A&P and get a candy bar. When I rush back, Mrs Gaspin is gone. *I can smell her on him.* How can you smell someone on someone else? Smell her like a fart, or what? I thought only dogs went around smelling people. I sense without knowing that there is an entire world inside that sentence. For years, after a date that would include some grappling, I would sniff the front of my own T-shirt, to see if I could smell my date.

Mom is staring up at the acoustic tiles through her cigarette smoke. I don't ask what's going on, because it will be none of my business. Then, I can't help myself.

'What's wrong with Mrs Gaspin?'

'She's divorced.'

'But it's Mrs Gaspin. She's always been divorced.'

My mother picks up a *Woman's Day* magazine. It's from Thanksgiving; the cover turkey is sun-bleached from sitting in the laundro window.

Without looking up, she says, 'Why don't you go in the bathroom and wash your elbows.'

3

On Exatitis

Being an ex, which means, obviously, having an ex, and then, further down the road, falling in love with another ex-spouse with an ex of his or her own, and a full complement of children and ex-in-laws, makes you wish you'd paid more attention in high school algebra. You realize, only after it's too late, that you never understood the true definition of the word 'exponential'. Don't try to make up for lost time: the dictionary definition, 'of, or relating to, an exponent' is no help at all. In any case, you're already living the real-life application. While you, Madame Ex, thought you were getting involved with Monsieur Ex, you were really getting involved with all the people from Monsieur's former marriage, many of whom still have it in for him in a way that is bound to eventually include you. This isn't double trouble, but trouble squared or trouble cubed.

Recently, I attended a wedding in a suburb of San Diego. It was the second for the bride, Celia (38), a short brunette who collects vintage European advertising posters and has one of those new-economy jobs where her job title is something whimsical like 'Head of Office Fun' (she works in human resources), and the third for Marcus (37), also short and dark, who composes music for television shows. Celia is divorced from Ian (38), with whom she has two children, Elizabeth (12) and Stephen (10). Marcus is divorced from Sandy (42), his first wife, and Anne (32), his second wife. He has a daughter, Amanda (15), with Sandy, and twin sons, Zack and Jake (6), with Anne.

Celia and Marcus had the wedding they've always wanted, one of the advantages of remarriage. Since it was her second and his third, their respective parents no longer had the energy, or the right, to insist on the inclusion of an ill-tempered third cousin in the wedding party, or to argue about the guest list or complain incessantly about the canapés. It was a black-and-white wedding. The children wore black velvet, even though it was Southern California in September, and thus eight thousand degrees in the shade. Elizabeth was the flower girl (at age twelve she thought she was a little old for that and sulked); Zack and Jake were both ring bearers (or ring losers, as Marcus joked). Stephen was the head usher. Amanda, an aspiring rock star, consented to be conned into singing 'Ave Maria.'

There was a swing band at the reception, a 'surf and turf' buffet, and a honeymoon in Fiji.

Celia knew this marriage would be different from the one with Ian – Ian was aloof and judgmental, while Marcus was warm and sloppy and tolerant to a fault – but assumed it would be similar in structure, with herself and Marcus at the center, their love blazing like the sun, with the children in orbit around them.

She envisioned it like this:

elizabeth   amanda

Celia + Marcus

stephen   jake & zack

Celia was wrong. Celia forgot to do her math. Instead, her marriage looked more like this:

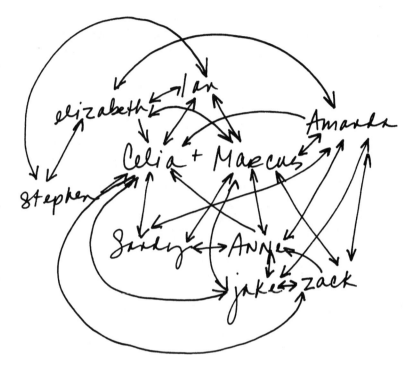

Celia loves Marcus.

Celia's first husband, Ian, is angry at Celia for having divorced him, but still loves her, and prides himself on being cordial in front of their children. He and Celia have joint custody. He is not just punctual; sometimes he's early bringing the kids home. He pays for new shoes and haircuts without being asked. Ian is thus getting a bit miffed that no one appreciates how decent he's being, when he could easily treat Celia like the traitorous slut he knows her to be. There was that rock climber between him and Marcus that he's sure Marcus doesn't know about. Heh heh.

Marcus's first wife, Sandy, despises Celia for taking Marcus away from his second wife, Anne, who may have been one of those arty-farty fruitcakes (a textile artist, Sandy doesn't even know what that means), but at least had provided a stable home for Amanda. Sandy does not have custody of Amanda because Marcus, the son of a bitch, took Amanda away when Sandy was going through sort of a bad patch. Sure, there was that credit card fraud thing (it was *not* her fault) and the eviction, but that didn't mean she wasn't a good mother.

Marcus's second wife, Anne, still pines for Marcus, says to herself once a day, *once an hour!*, that their divorce was all her fault. All her fault. She shouldn't have been so clingy. She shouldn't have been so jealous. She shouldn't have taken off her clothes on the front lawn and set them on fire after that party, but Marcus had refused to listen to her. (She is embarrassed to admit that she's since forgotten what the argument was about.) Anne reserves her wrath for Sandy, for having been such a pathetic excuse for a mother, and for saddling her, Anne, with that belligerent Amanda for all those years when Sandy was 'trying to get on her feet', and thus further stressing her fragile marriage to Marcus. The rage Anne feels for Celia is murderous. On her morning runs Anne fantasizes about what it would feel like to have her hands around Celia's neck. It makes Anne, who is small, with pointy shoulders and narrow hands, think she knows how men must feel. She controls herself through long, daily sessions of yoga and Wellbutron.

Amanda hates her own mother, Sandy, but mostly because she let her live with Anne, who was always kissy-sweet to Amanda in front of her dad, then yelled at her the second Dad turned his back. Celia, 'the current mother figure', is okay, but only so long as she stays out of the way. Amanda adores Marcus, her father. None of this was his fault. Celia's daughter, Elizabeth, has a really big ass.

Celia's daughter, Elizabeth, also worships her father, Ian, and is furious with her mother, and hates Marcus. Amanda is cool, though. She gets to wear nail polish with sparkles in it.

Stephen, Celia's son, doesn't think about it, and has developed a twitch, and cries a lot for no reason.

Marcus's twin sons, Zack and Jake, don't know who this new woman is, but she's nice enough. Except she keeps calling them Zack and Jack. They are afraid of this older boy named Stephen, who, when ordered to draw their baths, makes the water really hot and forces them to get in.

Marcus loves Celia, but secretly feels, as he did with Anne, that making all these relationships jibe is one of the things she needs to do. Who knows better than he, Marcus, how overbearing Sandy can be, how schizo Anne can be? That's why he divorced them. If Celia doesn't like them calling, she can just not answer the phone.

After the honeymoon, Celia develops a disliking not for Marcus, her beloved, but for Anne and Sandy, his ex-wives.

There are two basic types of ex: ex A and ex B.

Ex A is the ex who can't abide his or her own ex (in our model blended family Marcus and Sandy despise each other; Marcus also dislikes Anne).

Ex B is the ex who can't abide the new partner of her ex, or the ex of her new partner (Anne and Celia both like Marcus, and hate each other. Sandy, Anne, and Celia all hate each other; Ian isn't wild about Marcus and vice versa).

Exatitis A (as in hepatitis A) is relatively straightforward: You loathe while continuing to love the one who left you, usually for someone else, and you alternate between wanting to murder him and wanting to get him back. Although you are angrier than you've ever been in your

life, and the blinding glare of the anger – no, the rage!
– never dims, no matter how many kick-boxing classes
you take, no matter how many other lovers you take (so,
there), no matter how long you are on Prozac, you are
nevertheless blessed with some impulse control (unless
you're not, in which case you become the embittered
New Zealand ex-husband who bludgeoned his ex-wife
to death with a pound of frozen sausage). So instead
of homicide, you opt for milder forms of retribution. I
know one woman who ordered a subscription of *Hustler*
sent to her husband's office. I know another who tried
to give her ex-husband food poisoning by inviting him
to dinner and serving hamburger that had been thawed
once and refrozen. Her mother had warned her against
this her entire adult life; you could die from it. The
ex-husband neither died nor suffered even a mild case of
heartburn. Nearly everyone else I've queried who suffers
from exatitis A, both male and female, has run up every
credit card left over from the marriage.

You are beyond furious about being forced to become
an ex against your will (perhaps it was your decision, and
you're angry about having made it), and everything your
ex does from the point of the divorce onward is icing
on the cake, an odd saying meant to give the impression
that this something else is something extra. Not true. Do
you know any child (children being the main cake eaters
in this world) who prefers the cake over the icing? The

icing is a full partner in the cake-eating experience, just as everything your ex does pisses you off.

She left you, *and now she's taking a night class in landscape design!*

He left you, *and now he's putting a deck on the back of the house!*

He or she left you, *and now he or she is dating Fill In the Blank!* (Every mammal on earth is objectionable.)

He's breathing in and out, that rat!

Like hepatitis A, which is contracted from the salad bar at a restaurant where someone has failed to heed that sign in the washroom about washing hands, the cause of exatitis A is pretty obvious. She done you wrong. You have every right to be insane with indignation and hatred.

Exatitis B is more complex. Like hepatitis B, you're not sure where you got it, intercourse and injections being the main culprits, but people who haven't had sex or a tetanus shot since the age of skinny ties have been known to contract it too.

You believe yourself to be a logical, rational, reasonable ex. You get along well enough with your ex-husband or ex-wife, the person who was at one time closer to you than anyone else, and who presumably has hurt you better and harder than anyone else.

No, the person you've conceived a nearly Homeric hatred for is the ex-wife of your new love, a woman who almost undoubtedly has a full-blown, rampaging case of exatitis B herself. If you marry your new love, you gain not simply a new mother-in-law and father-in-law, you also get this person who won't rest until you're at least as miserable as she is. She is your ex-wife-in-law.

The troubled relationship between the second – or third – wife and her husband's ex-wife – or wives – is a relatively new development in the brave new, no-fault divorce world. It goes without saying that ex-wives and ex-husbands dislike each other. Otherwise, they'd still be married. But studies do show that ex-spouses without children get along much better than ex-spouses who've had children together.

A magazine editor I know whose wife left him for his best friend ten years ago feels no rancor for her. 'When I try to reassemble what happened with Denise, I can get myself worked up. She left me, saying she was going to rent her own apartment, saying she needed time to think. She said she was going to be staying in a nearby hotel for a while. She wasn't lying. She was at the hotel. With my best friend. It was all sort of tawdry and dramatic. But when I think about her now, it's with the same affection I reserve for any old girlfriend. We were young adults together. We didn't know what the hell we were doing. We had some good times. I haven't seen her since the day she came and got her furniture. I remarried happily and have a daughter, and she remarried my friend and I've heard is with him still. So I guess it was all meant to be.'

My friend is able to hold fond feelings for his ex because, to put it bluntly, she's not in his face day in, day out, the way she might be if they had a passel of underage children they were trying to parent. He is able to feel nostalgic for her because she is gone. It's no stretch for him to put the marriage behind him.

Prior to the decade between 1966 and 1976, when the divorce rate doubled and women began leaving their marriages in greater numbers, the ex-husband usually paid for leaving by . . . leaving. It went unsaid that he was giving up not just his marriage, but also his children. No one supposed in those days that a father did much but bring home the proverbial bacon. It hadn't been proven that a child needed a sustained relationship with both natural parents. No one had heard of so-called fathers' rights, including the father. Indeed, until recently it was legal in most states for the mother to withhold visitation if the father wasn't current on his child support.

In those Mom-raises-the-kids, Dad-makes-the-money-and-the-martinis days, there were no books with titles like *Fathering: Strengthening the Connection with Your Children No Matter Where You Are* or *101 Ways to Be a Special Dad,* no Internet sites like dadmag.com, which calls itself 'the real home for dads', who are 'members of the Great Ignored'. (There was no Internet, but you get the picture.) Robert Bly was not yet out in the woods beating his drum and longing for the day when the word 'fathering' would conjure up the same cuddly feelings of warmth and nurturing that the word 'mothering' does.

While divorce rates have remained more or less steady over the last few decades, the number of fathers who are determined to play an active role in their children's lives has grown. Most dads today want a piece of the parental action in the way our fathers never did. Even the workaholics are up for reading bedtime stories, chauffeuring their kids to gymnastics when they can, shopping for school clothes, helping out in the classroom. They want to be involved. They want to know that Petey is allergic to strawberries and Polly still likes to sleep with the light on. They like to know these things even if they're divorced. Even if they're remarried.

The old-style divorced dad might remarry, but he would start a new family and rarely, if ever, see the old one. The new-style involved and remarried dad wants all the kids to play together. And why not? The problem is, of course, there is his new wife, and his ex-wife.

They do not want to play together.

I had known Matthew for six months before the Underpants Episode. I still supposed I was exatitis free. I thought I was above all that Jerry Springer behavior (tune in later to see me pull the phone out of the wall and throw it out the back door). I had my own shining joint custody agreement with my ex-husband as evidence I was symptomless for exatitis A. We'd never argued once in front of our daughter, which made us proud of ourselves (we'd never argued in our marriage, either, which sort of made our accomplishment less spectacular than it sounds).

As for exatitis B, there was no reason I should feel anything but charitable toward Claudia, who after all had lost a good man. Matthew had also assured me their split had been amicable. Or rather, he hedged. When I asked, 'Who left whom?' he said, 'Depends on who you talk to. And have I told you how much I love a woman who still believes in using *whom*? Do you also churn your own butter?'

Later, Matthew would admit that he said that to all the girls. Not the flirtatious whom/butter churning business, but the part that makes it sound as if he and Claudia had talked reasonably and prudently about ending their marriage, then sadly decided it was time, as if they were taking an old cat to the vet to be put down, instead of what really happened, which was Matthew finally shouting that he couldn't take it anymore and trying to leave, but getting stuck on the threshold of their apartment because Claudia was hanging on to his ankles, biting at the cuffs of his pants. Matthew admitted that like most guys he wasn't above using confession as a tool of seduction, but felt that telling me, or any of the other women he'd dated, the real circumstances of his divorce would not achieve the desired result. Which, of course, was to get laid.

Except for me! He didn't know me well enough to know that as much as I found the above scene horrifying, I was also fascinated, as would be any woman who as a girl was given books with titles like *White Gloves and Party Manners*.

I was moved not so much by Claudia's masterful inability to control herself, but by her assumption that whatever she hurled – including, according to Matthew, car keys, ice cream cones, lawn furniture, epithets – she was not to be held accountable for it. Her tantrums were never to be held against her, never to be cited by Matthew, her ex-husband, or anyone else, as a reason for being angry at her or for shunning her. Being Claudia meant never having to say you're sorry. And she didn't. I admire that kind of self-righteousness in a person. Not to mention the lack of embarrassment.

Watching Claudia conduct her life, I felt like one of the extras in *Saturday Night Fever*, in the famous scene where John Travolta in his gangsterish white suit spins and poses and throws out that slender, surly hip, raising disco dancing to the next level. I'm one of the onlookers too self-conscious to draw that much attention to herself.

I remember one late-night phone call with Matthew that was a chronicle of the Underpants Episode foretold. It was 11:40 (digital clocks with their blocky, glowing red letters have done wonders for accurately identifying the exact time the body was discovered, and otherwise aiding the power of memory). One of Matthew's more charming qualities is his ability to talk on the phone longer than a teenage girl. He thought about his students a lot, and we'd talk about them as if they were characters in a soap opera. He was telling me about one girl who amazed him: she spent the entire class putting on eye shadow and talking on her baby lavender cell phone (in class??), then turned in perfect papers. 'This is a girl who understands the meaning of a topic sentence, and knows the difference between "lay" and "lie",' he said.

'Ah, another butter churner,' I said. 'I bet she sews her own clothes.'

Then I heard some commotion in the background, a door thudding shut in the distance, a second of silence, then a cascade of human-sounding squawks and bleats, followed by the unmistakable sound of clothes being yanked in bunches from a closet, the metal-against-wood *riiiiiiiip* of hangers being dragged across the wooden bar, the cheesy clatter of their plastic shoulders. Matthew said, 'I have to go,' and hung up. I heard something in his voice I hadn't heard before. Fear.

I would later find out the reason Claudia felt inspired

to walk into her ex-husband's house at 11:40 on a Sunday night and remove all the clothes he'd been gallantly storing for her at the back of his closet, but at the moment I was completely confused.

A digression here: Matthew felt he owed Claudia access to his superior closet, which covered an entire wall, since it was because of the divorce that she was forced to make do with her own vastly inferior closet. The fact that Claudia was forced to deal with a vastly inferior closet fed directly into Matthew's guilt. And perhaps he should have felt guilty. Statistically, men do much better financially after divorce than do women. The standard of living for ex-husbands goes up while that of ex-wives goes down, although it's not the dramatic variation it's been made out to be. The myth is that the first year after the divorce the ex-wife's standard of living drops 73 per cent while the ex-husband's rises 42 per cent; in fact, hers drops about 25 per cent while his rises 10 per cent.

No matter. It hardly applied to Matthew and Claudia. She still used his credit cards, and at the end of the month he deposited any spare cash directly into her checking account.

The closet in her single-bedroom apartment was smaller than a phone booth, with no room for a large royal-blue down jacket too warm for any climate south of Juneau, or the useless bridesmaid dress worn once, the smaller skirts and trousers that Claudia was probably waiting to shrink into (I'm assuming this because every woman I know has these), the flimsy gold plastic garment bag with a white cursive *C* stitched on it, a pathetic nod to gentility.

Matthew, who had initiated their divorce a mere eighteen months after they were married on impulse in Reno, lived in Levi's 501s and T-shirts when he wasn't wearing the khakis and cotton pastel button-downs that he wore to work, and had plenty of closet space, which Claudia felt it was her right to colonize. And so she did, and so he let her. Until that night, when she marched in and stripped his closet of all those useless clothes, punishing him for the fact that earlier in the day Matthew had mentioned in passing that he had been cut out of his parents' will. (Why? What did he do? I never found out.)

Perhaps this scenario makes sense to you. Maybe if you learned that your ex-husband had been cut out of your ex-in-laws' will (which you weren't included in for obvious reasons), you would also be swept up in righteous indignation, enough to pitch a middle-of-the-night fit and deprive your ex of the satisfaction of storing clothes you never wore in a part of his closet he never looked in, but for me, well, the whole thing was gloriously perplexing.

All I could figure was this: Claudia had somehow been counting on the small amount of money that would pass to Matthew and then down to Erica. In about sixty years. If there was anything to pass down. And now that Matthew (and, by extension, Claudia and her child) was disowned, she would pay Matthew's parents back by disowning their son's closet. At 11:40 on a Sunday night.

I was dazzled.

For a few weeks I thought it would be cool if Claudia and I could be pals, or whatever word falls between 'acquaintance' and 'friend'. I must have picked up this notion from Kiki, a gregarious soul who has an impressive habit of befriending the exes of her current love, and, more astonishing still, the exes of her exes. This philosophy was an offshoot of all that free love business in the 1960s and 1970s. When you loved the one you were with, it was a given that there would be exes. Many exes. All those other chicks with whom your new old man had done it in the road. Being jealous or resentful of them was not in keeping with the free love credo, not to mention it being so establishment, or whatever they called it.

Kiki made a lot of great women friends that way. The boyfriend would inevitably become the ex-boyfriend and drift away, but Kiki would remain buddies with the ex-boyfriend's ex-girlfriend, because now they had even more in common, both being exes of the same guy. The two of *them* could get together for a drink after work and reminisce about old times with Richard without having to involve Richard himself. Remember how he used to tug on his eyelid when he was nervous? Remember how he never liked to spend Friday night, but would happily spend Saturday night? What was *that* about? And what about his euphemism for being in the mood for sex: *Hey, babe, there's no cover charge tonight at Club Zucchini.* Kiki got to have the fond memories of the love affair without risking rekindling it by calling the onetime love object and suggesting they get together for 'old times' sake' (which leads to more unplanned pregnancies than you might imagine).

I realize as I write this that the reverse is also true: Nothing signals the final seconds of a love affair like a post-game wrap-up with one of his exes. It's over for you, yes, but also over for the ex. This is probably the true reason I wanted to make Claudia's acquaintance. Her willingness to meet me for a cup of coffee some Saturday morning, or maybe sit together and watch the kids play at one of Erica's birthday parties (an event to which I was never fortunate enough to receive an invitation. Her words to Matthew were something along the lines of, 'bring that whore and you'll regret it'), would signal that she had moved on, that she no longer hated (i.e., loved) Matthew, but only disliked (i.e., liked) him.

I thought our meeting would be kind of sporting, like the winner hopping over the net to shake the hand of the loser of a tennis match, which, come to think of it, I've never actually seen anyone do. The winner may approach the net to give his condolences to the loser, but the hopping-over part seems to demand too much in the way of high jumping skills, or else the risk of being marooned for a minute or so straddling the net.

I assumed that it would be easy to arrange a meeting with Claudia so that I could display my friendly impulses. Wouldn't she be as interested in checking me out as I was in checking her out? I knew she was fat; she knew I was old (six years older than Matthew; *eleven* years older than her). Wouldn't my appraisal of her big bottom and her appraisal of my crows' feet give us both a nice, cream-filled bonbon with which to comfort ourselves when on some endless lonely night she was bemoaning the fact that Matthew had chosen me over her (even though they had been divorced for four years, it would always seem to her that he had left her for me), and when on some endless lonely night I was bemoaning the fact that even though Matthew claimed to be in love with me, he was still emotionally entangled with her? Wouldn't knowing each other be satisfying for us both?

I met Matthew when I was a visiting writer in his classroom for a week. It was mild interest at first sight, but by the end of the week I was blushing like one of his female students and calling him by his last name, as if I were a Jane Austen heroine. 'Mr Locke, how are you today? When you're done with your character sketches students, please pass them to Mr Locke.'

One of the things I found most attractive was the way he conducted himself in his classroom. He had forty-two kids in an eleventh-grade English class, and three of them were already parents. The rest seemed to have siblings still in diapers, and one boy lived in a family where none of the four children had the same father. There was a beautiful Laotian girl who had been married at twelve and was already a divorced single mother. Matthew refused to dumb his syllabus down for them simply because they had other problems; he wasn't going to pretend rock lyrics were art, or rappers were poets, or any of the other things desperate teachers do to try to engage their students. Matthew made them read and write about *A Tale of Two Cities* just as he would any other captives of the public school system, and I think they appreciated it. They complained, they made excuses for not finishing their work, but they showed up for class and tried to limit the back talk.

When I suggested to Matthew that I call Claudia to see if she wanted to get together, he was a different person. Nervous. Slouchy. His normal movie-trailer-narrator voice went up an octave. The whites of his blue eyes turned pink; he munched on his upper lip. 'That's not a good idea.'

I had a bad feeling. 'You have told her about us, haven't you?'

'Well, I haven't kept you a secret,' he said.

Hedge, hedge, hedge.

I suddenly remembered one day several months earlier when Matthew asked me to stay in the bathroom while Claudia came over to pick up a sleeping bag for a slumber party Erica had been invited to. We were getting ready to go out somewhere – I can't remember where – and the phone rang. Naturally, it was Claudia. It was never not Claudia. Even though Matthew was reputed to have friends, no one ever called but Claudia. At least not while I was around.

Matthew didn't actually say, 'Go hide in the bathroom.' He sort of waved his nice backstroker's arm toward the back of the house and said, 'Maybe, I don't know, she'll only be here for a minute. If you could . . .'

A real Jane Austen heroine would never have agreed to it. She would have said, 'Hide? Are you kidding?' and thrown open the door, sleeping bag under her arm, willing, indeed ready, to have it out there on the front porch. Or, she would have said, 'Look, until you're ready to make sure your ex-wife knows you're in love with someone else, I'm outta here!'

But I'm not heroine material, much as I would like to be. Don't have the necessary purity of heart, faith in humanity, wasp waist, or bee-stung lips. Instead, I offered, *offered*, to stand for a good fifteen minutes in the windowless bathroom, bits of cobweb and towel lint stuck on the dingy white walls, which were perpetually moist from the last shower, the fan on the fritz, the linoleum still slick as well.

It's possible that I did it just so I would have it to fling in his face during hundreds of subsequent fights: '*You made me hide in the bathroom! How was that supposed to make me feel?*'

I refolded the towels. I plucked my eyebrows. Then I thought, I am thirty-seven years old. I have a three-year-old daughter. I have a fledgling career as an adventure and travel writer. *Am I out of my mind?* To which the answer was, *Yes, I am out of my mind.* I could truly say, 'I'd rather jump off a bridge (I have; in a bungee-jumping story) than face Claudia.'

In Matthew's defense – how many times have women in love used that phrase? – he had tried to tell her about us. Sort of. Let's say he strongly hinted. He said he said, for example, 'Karen and I are really getting close.' If someone said this to me, I would immediately think, *Close? What do you mean, 'close'?! Are you telling me you're in love with her?!* Not Claudia. I admired her heel-grinding refusal to accept reality when it didn't suit her, her determination not to heed her intuition. She has the makings of a great polar explorer, possessing as she does the ability to refuse to accept defeat, to press on when all is lost.

One day she stood in the middle of the driveway and said to Matthew: 'I love you, I'll always love you. Do you know how much I love you? More than you know. That's how much I love you!'

Matthew feigned a sudden interest in a crack in the concrete that looked as if it might be housing a colony of ants. In his capacity as a teacher (always learning!), he could do this once in a while and get away with it. Then he said, 'Well, guess I'll talk to you later.'

Most women understand all too well this tactful changing of the subject. Claudia is more like an Army recruiter: He didn't say he *didn't* love me, so that means he must. She will not think otherwise until she hears, 'I don't love you. I will never love you again. Do you have any idea how much I don't love you? I'd like to maim you for life, that's how much I don't love you.' You need to say this two inches from her nose, in the same way you might address a dog who's just chewed your shoe. Matthew did not have the heart or the guts to do this.

Near the end of our love affair, I would one day shove Matthew across the kitchen for his repeated failure to make his feelings for me clear to her, but that came later. Now I thought: Naturally he's reluctant to be straight with her. Who in his right mind would willingly provoke someone like Claudia, with her history of kicking in the kitchen cabinets? Not to mention biting. Once, she bit Matthew so hard he needed a tetanus shot.

It's also possible Matthew never told Claudia a thing.

4

All Rage, All the Time

After the Underpants Episode, my feelings for Claudia changed. I didn't think it would be so sporting of me to know her any more. I believed her when she told Matthew she was going to spend the rest of her life making my life a living hell. I am not one of those people who thinks bad things happen only to other people. I harbor a superstitious belief that by trusting something will never happen to me, I am inviting fate to correct my assumption. And I was learning that strange things happened to exes. There was a woman somewhere in Indiana whose ex-husband came over on Valentine's Day and tried to shoot her with a crossbow. That one's gotta catch a girl by surprise.

After I found the contents of my overnight case all over Matthew's bathroom, I salvaged what I could, threw out the rest, went back into the bedroom and turned my duffel bag right-side out, tossed in my clothes, and said, 'I'm going somewhere else tonight.' I had no real idea where, although I knew there would be something Marriott-related off I-5. I would have called Kiki, but she was in Florida visiting her parents while the floors were being refinished.

I expected Matthew to stop me. I imagined a television-style argument in which I would say, trembling and trying not to cry, 'She's got your keys and she's already threatened to kill me once. She's capable of anything!'

He would then take me in his arms and try to jolly me out of my fear by saying something about her bark being worse than her bite, or that she really didn't mean it – some typical male dissembling – to which the only response would be my hurling my cut-up underpants in his face.

None of that happened, which, paradoxically, should have made me feel better, should have made me feel that I was not overreacting, that I was right. Instead, Matthew agreed with me. Not reassuring at all.

'I'm coming with you,' he said.

This was how we wound up spending the night at a Holiday Inn Express not ten miles away from where we both lived.

There were fewer than a dozen cars in the parking lot; the place was nearly empty. Matthew gallantly put the room on his Visa. This scenario was ludicrous, unless

Claudia returned to the house later thinking she could murder us in our sleep. Then it was prudent.

While we were checking in, Matthew said, 'You're probably surprised by all this. I am not surprised. I should have told you sooner. I should have told you.'

I then heard about how Claudia had tried to kill herself by driving into a concrete wall, except not really, because she was wearing a seat belt and going only twenty-five miles an hour. I got the greatest hits of all the property damage in the name of love. I learned that Claudia once tore up an entire basket of laundry because Matthew wouldn't fold it when she asked him to. I learned that Lillian, Claudia's mother, used to beat Claudia with a rake. I also learned that Lillian had a police record, for embezzling funds from the car dealership where she'd once worked.

'You mean she's done time?' I said.

Matthew said no, or he didn't know, really, it happened way before he'd met Claudia, back when she was in junior high school. It was for Claudia's horseback riding lessons.

'Horseback riding lessons? Her mother committed a felony so her daughter could take horseback riding lessons?'

Why this seemed worse than everything else, I didn't know. I did know that my instant and pronounced disdain revealed exactly the limitations of my left-leaning political sentiments. I could understand risking jail time to prevent being evicted, or to pay for medical care, or even Christmas. But horseback riding lessons?

In our room, Matthew's cell phone shivered spastically on the dresser. He'd turned the ringer off, but left it on vibrate. Every few minutes it went off, then lay there silent, as though it had not one more twitch in it, then started quivering all over again, a roadkill not quite dead. A few rooms over, a man was singing loudly, ardently, in Spanish. Not karaoke, this. No phony sentiment. Someone's heart was breaking down the hall.

It was free cable night at the motel. Matthew and I sat propped against the phony headboard, attached to the wall but not to the bed. The air-conditioner was an overachiever. We were forced to warm ourselves beneath the polyester bedspread, the part of a hotel room that is the most loaded with germs and other nasties, since it's never changed and rarely washed.

We watched *It Could Happen to You*, the romantic comedy starring Nicolas Cage and Bridget Fonda, about a waitress and a cop who win the lottery, or maybe it's the cop who wins the lottery and gives half of it to the waitress. Although it's based on a true story, it was utterly unbelievable.

Once a year, for a week in the summer, I teach a writing class called 'Fiction Writing for the Restless'. My students are generally more talented than I, but have a terrible time simply sitting down and writing. On the first day I give them my rule: I never want to hear, 'but it really happened!' to justify weak writing. Something really happening is irrelevant. I don't care if it really happened.

Sitting cuddled under the slippery bedspread watching *It Could Happen to You*, while Matthew's phone went nuts and I found myself listening for sirens and wondering if Claudia had returned to the scene of the crime and the house was now in flames, I realized this pronouncement is a little harsh of me. What my students want credited to their account is the gravity of the event. Something happened to change things. Their mistake is not in whining, 'But it really happened,' but in striving to make it seem logical.

I tried to do my old thought trick, describing my situation to myself as if I were a stranger. I'm a thirty-seven-year-old woman with a three-year-old daughter and no real job, being forced to seek safe refuge in a cheesy motel from a woman who says she wants to kill me because I'm in love with her ex-husband.

It could happen to you.

The next morning Matthew's house was still there, no broken windows or soot-blackened walls. There were many colorful phone messages, which Matthew's room-mates were used to and had ignored, as they always did. I was surprised that only about half of the calls were from Claudia herself; the others were from Lillian, issuing dazzling prosecutable threats. Lillian's messages accused Matthew of ruining her daughter's life. She promised through a hurricane of tears that she would make sure that both he and his home-wrecking slut would pay, and pay dearly. Claudia's messages were weeping, stuffy-nosed pleas. 'Eeyore, please don't be mad at your bouncy Tigger. You know how Tiggers are. We can't help ourselves. We're so, so bouncy. Please.'

I must stop right here. I want legislation. When a marriage dies, all those cloying nicknames that signified your private world should die with it. Like a secret family recipe for the foolproof soufflé that goes to the grave with the auntie who perfected it, or the codes to secret missions that expire with the spy, all the Sweet Cheeks and Wuver Boys, the Tweetie Pies and Peachie Weachies and Big Bucko-Wuckos, the Winkys and the Binkys and every other lame-o term of endearment should never be spoken aloud after you've split. I know from experience that you stand a good chance of scaring away a future partner when he discovers that you were once known as Foxy Mamakins.

Until that moment I hadn't known Claudia and Matthew had Tigger and Eeyore as their alter egos, and at one time had liked to pretend they lived in the Hundred Acre Wood with all the other overmerchandised Milne characters. (This from a man who, when I told him I'd finally gotten around to reading *Middlemarch*, sighed and said it was the only Eliot he hadn't yet reread.) The idea I may have fallen in a love with a full-grown man and father of one who allowed himself to be referred to as Eeyore made my molars ache. The men I had loved before Matthew thought that calling your beloved 'Honey' was the epitome of drooling sentimentality, and I had therefore been trained to steer clear of sappy endearments, not to mention corny ones.

Whoever got the Tigger-Eeyore thing going – please, please, make it be Claudia, who is tacky and unoriginal and without a molecule of irony – had mistaken all things Winnie-the-Pooh for something fresh, original, evocative of an inner, intimate world, when in fact it was part of the collective consciousness of millions of consumers who had all had the same thought. Drop by any mall or movieplex in America and there will be hundreds of women in Tigger T-shirts and men in Eeyore baseball caps, all women and men, presumably, who believe they are clever for discovering their inner Piglet.

I thought about the Tigger-Eeyore thing quite a bit, as I'm sure Claudia intended me to. Indeed, after Matthew and I had moved in together (you didn't think the Underpants Episode was the end, did you? Never forget, calamity brings people together. Until, of course,

it drives them apart) there was still the occasional letter addressed to Matthew from 'Tiggerrrrrrrr!' Yuck.
Oh, and of course, I was jealous. I consoled myself by
reassuring myself that Claudia was dense enough to miss
the subtext of her self-endearment. Setting aside the fact
that few people have less spring in their step than the
bovine Claudia, she-as-Tigger, Matthew-as-Eeyore was
an unwittingly accurate metaphor for their relationship.
Like the tiger with the spring in his tail, she trounced,
flounced, bounced, and pounced, jumped, clumped, and
thumped while her husband, then her ex-husband, in the
role of the gloomy Eeyore, ducked.

Matthew finally answered the phone around noon.
When there is a six-year-old child between you, in
the end you always answer the phone. Before Matthew
answered, he asked me to listen to make sure he didn't say
anything too forgiving, and to tell him when five minutes
were up. This made me feel as if I were an FBI agent
overseeing a phone call to a kidnapper, or the other way
around, a kidnapper having the obligatory ransom chat
with the FBI.

I wish I could report that I said, 'No way! You're on
your own!'

I leaned against the doorjamb of his neat, nearly empty
bedroom, so bereft of decor it always made me love him
a little more whenever I saw it, listening to the break
in his voice as he said, 'I know you want to be a good

girl.' After ten minutes I got impatient and said, loudly, 'I think they call it breaking and entering. Have her ask her mother. I'm sure she'd know.'

Later, Claudia came over and Matthew went and sat in her car with her, trying to make her feel better about having behaved so badly, while I waited in his bedroom. I sat on the edge of his bed and read a book.

Some sociologists have built entire careers on the study of anger and rage, and have discovered through mammoth, decades-long studies and complex research models what all ex-spouses learn after the first big post-divorce argument: There's no statute of limitations on wanting to strangle someone.

Time does not heal all wounds, and never has. The person who began this rumor was clearly an optimist who tried to heal the wound in question in a more traditionally proactive fashion. He went on a drunken binge, joined the military, got involved with a milkmaid from the next village who managed to inflict yet one more wound that needed healing. He tried everything, then fell on time as being the great wound-healer because the next line of reasoning – *nothing* will heal this wound – would portend the advent of existentialism, and this saying is much older than Sartre.

Part of being human is having wounds that will never heal. There are wounds you may take to your grave.

There are wounds that are less like cutting your finger with a knife (frantic trip to ER with towel wrapped around hand, six stitches, Tylenol with codeine, the eventual thin white scar) and more like a hernia that opens up every time you do any heavy lifting. And to extend this rather forced metaphor, in this case the heavy lifting is thinking about not simply your ex, but about anything that goes wrong in your life, because everything becomes his fault. If he hadn't left you, you would not have stubbed your toe on the dining room table leg and kicked the cat. If he hadn't wanted a divorce, you would be able to afford that mountain bike you always wanted. If you were still married to your ex your child wouldn't have dyed his hair blue, or flunked U.S. history, or decided not to go to college.

For some exes time not only fails to heal the wound, but causes it to fester, like Henry VIII's oozing, icky leg wound. For some exes things get worse over time because time in this case is not a balm, but a creative writing grant that allows for the composition of an elaborate Dostoevskian narrative of blame and intrigue, an ongoing saga of betrayal that begins with the initial request for a divorce and is large enough in scope to encompass everything the ex does for the rest of his life. The narrative is written, then rehearsed. Over and over again. She – or he, although usually it's an ex-wife – will tell her tale of woe to any one who'll listen. When I was gathering stories for this book I would sit down to interview someone and say, 'Tell me about your ex-husband,' and wouldn't need to say another word. It was as if I'd flipped a switch.

'You should have seen the tie he wore to Jennifer's piano recital. That was the tie he wore on our third date. He knew I would remember. He doesn't think I feel bad enough? He had to wear that tie?

'Last week he was ON TIME to pick up the kids. Can you believe it? What a schmuck. He's always been late before. Now suddenly he has a new squeeze and he wants to show her what a terrific father he is? That he can actually get his ass over to my house to pick up his children on time? He's just doing that to get my goat.

'And what about that new girlfriend? Isn't she a skinny nag? A fat hag? What's with the teeth? What's with the two arms and two legs? What's with that way she talks by opening and closing her mouth? That bitch.'

This ability to keep yourself angry seemingly forever has to do with the Lasagna Model of Emotional Stress. To understand it, we need to start with the bottom layer, the spicy tomato sauce that forms the basis of the dish: romantic love.

Much of what we talk about when we talk about love is self-love. Virginia Woolf informed us that woman's natural function is to act as a mirror that reflects man back at twice his normal size. Men do a lot of reflecting back as well, by telling us we look great: young, sexy, smart. Whatever it is we want to hear, we get to hear it when we're newly in love.

Prior to meeting your future beloved, you're bobbing along with only your own self-perception to keep you on an even keel. Suddenly, there is someone who thinks your habit of talking too much is charming; the bump on your nose gives you character; your tendency to dither is beguiling.

Someone else once said that love is a mutual agreement to overestimate each other's good points. Now you have somebody to turbo-charge your self-perception. It turns out you're the hottest babe on earth after all. Most of us never progress beyond sixth grade in the self-love department. When our mothers asked us why we got involved in the food fight in the cafeteria, we said it was because everyone else was doing it, and this is pretty much our standard response to self-love for the rest of our lives. As long as someone else loves us, we figure we'll give ourselves a shot, too.

We get married. Set up unreal expectations. Lay down the wide flat noodles in the baking dish over the spicy tomato sauce. I've recited the marriage vows from the Book of Common Prayer twice now, and have never failed to be moved to tears by their grandeur, their poetry. But let's face it, they appeal not so much to the part of us wanting to make a commitment (really, who wants to do that?), as to the infantile side that never wants things to change, never wants to be disappointed, never wants to be left alone. The side that stamps its foot and says, 'But you promised!' It's a lovely, poignant ceremony, but even the most stellar marriages end in the divorce that is death. As Dorothy Parker pointed out, there are no happy endings.

Add to the spicy tomato sauce of romantic love and the hearty noodles of marriage, the gooey, sweetish ricotta of married life, the feeling of security, companionship, the regular sex. Nice to share a bed with someone, too. The double income. Holidays are not just bearable, but fun. Travel is the adventure it should be. The wedding ring on your hand feels good.

Then one day your husband or wife tells you it's over. The person you were supposed to spend your life with is moving the boxes with his yearbooks in them out of the basement. They were supposed to stay there forever. The marriage vows said so. Maybe he or she already has someone else, which makes you think you know what a heart attack victim feels. You're shocked, and the feeling isn't temporary. You've never seen that vein stand out in the middle of your forehead before. Now you wouldn't recognize yourself without it.

Now someone else is enjoying the reflecting quality of your spouse. Your mirror's been lifted by someone else. You're humiliated. You're bereft. If you have children, you've also lost someone with whom to share the parenting. You've lost your companion. You've lost the other paycheck. You've lost a chance to extend the past into the future.

Feelings of betrayal, bitterness, grief, and despair at the severing of the marriage are then topped with feelings of betrayal and outrage and revenge brought on by the adversarial nature of divorce. The flavors complement one another. Everything accentuates the pain of everything else. A happy couple walking down the street reminds you that you no longer have that. A form letter from your attorney informing you of a change of address reminds you that you hate your ex. A friend who's seeing a man who's in the middle of a divorce is despicable for no other reason than the fact that your ex began seeing someone while he was divorcing you.

Pop in the oven.

Bake for the rest of your life.

Passengers don't talk on airplanes anymore. Five years ago if you sat next to someone who didn't want to talk, it was her responsibility to make busy gestures indicating that a conversation was unwelcome, whipping out the fat paperback before the door had even been closed, getting out the yellow pad and calculator and mechanical pencil. If the person just sat there, or even if she flipped through the in-flight magazine, it was a signal that you might safely say, 'Where are you headed?' without violating the seat mate's code of conduct. These days it's a given that conversation is as unwelcome as being wedged in the middle seat amongst a family of four. There is no talking, unless the person on the inside needs to get out to go to the bathroom.

I'm fine with this. I was probably one of the founders of the movement to stop in-flight chattering, for there is nothing worse than being stuck next to someone who has never learned the miracle of narrative summary. The shocker about Adele was that she didn't look like someone who would be an insane ex-wife. I should qualify that – she didn't look like a woman who would behave in a manner that people who weren't exes would perceive to be insane. There's a big difference.

Adele worked as a copy editor at a small company that made women's golf apparel, and wore the kind of demure Laura Ashley dress that I've often admired in windows, but have never been able to put on without feeling like a sofa in a flowered slipcover. She had chin-length blond hair, bangs, a beguiling yellowish capped front tooth.

While the flight attendant was doing the seat belt lecture Adele asked me where I was going and what I did, and when I said I was a writer she wondered who I wrote for and did I bring the stories to them or did they come to me and how did I get started and don't I feel lucky and isn't my life exciting? I told her that it can be great fun, except when it's a colossal drag. I told her I try to limit my trips to no more than three days, because I miss my little girl.

Adele wonders who Katherine stays with and when I tell her my ex-husband, that is the moment our bond is cemented for all eternity. *You have an ex, too?* Suddenly, we become two geezers who both suffered quadruple bypass surgery. We fought World War II together. We graduated from the same law school. We survived the same hurricane. Andrea Lee in her short story 'Interesting Women' describes the phenomenon thus: 'And then I drop the word "ex-husband" – that password that functions as a secret handshake in the freemasonry of interesting women.'

'Oh. God. Don't get me started,' Adele said. Too late, too late.

'I got laid off from my job, right? Not the job I have now, well, obviously not the job I have now, or else I wouldn't still have it, right? So I clean my desk and go home and walk into the house, and there's my husband in bed with my supervisor. In my own bed. In the middle of the day. This was the supervisor who called in sick that day and I thought it was because she didn't want to be the one to give me the bad news, when really what she wanted was to spend the day with my husband, who had also called in sick. They'd met at the company Christmas party. They didn't hear me come in, or maybe they did and they wanted me to see them, so they wouldn't have to tell me. I should have noticed her car, but what would Trudy be doing at my house in the middle of the day, you know? I walk into the bedroom, my own bedroom, and there they are, completely naked. Not even *in* my bed; *on* my bed, on the stupid suede percale duvet cover I ordered especially from some mail-order place trying to make our bedroom a special sanctuary just for sleeping and whatnot, just like they tell you to do, the sleep experts. And I'm still carrying the box with my junk from work and there's a picture of my husband in a frame staring right up at me, a picture of him with his stupid tumory eight-hundred-year-old Bernese mountain dog, and I was the one who always took it to the vet. I had it on my desk, this fucking picture of him and the dog. It wasn't the picture I liked best of him, but it was the picture he said represented him best. This is the type of narcissistic fucking asshole we're talking about here. What I want to know is, how did that become my fucking job, taking the fucking dog to the vet?'

Her voice was getting that edge that made me start thinking that any minute she'd start fumbling around in her shoulder bag for the plastic gun. Her cheeks were getting flushed. She'd shredded her napkin. I was kind of fascinated, since as I said, my own separation and divorce had been conducted in such a stately, elegiac fashion.

'So I'm staring at them, and they're *naked*. Trudy's actually staring somewhere to the right of my head, like at

the wall, like I'm not even *there* and my husband's back is
to me and I'm staring at his birthmark, on his butt. That's
all I can do, is stare at that stupid Argentina birthmark he's
got, this brown splotch that looks like Argentina. You'd
think they'd leap up and put their clothes on. I go back
out of the house and sit in the car. This wasn't the first
time with someone I knew, by the way. The asshole. The
cocksucker. The next day I throw all his stuff out on the
street, like I'm Italian or something. He moves in with
Trudy, that cunt, and then has the fucking nerve to ask
me to keep the fucking Bernese Mountain dog because
Trudy lives in an apartment and can't have pets. So he
wants to like have visitation with the fucking dog. So I
take the dog to the vet and I tell them to put the thing
down. That my husband and I had decided. The next
time he comes over – that's the other thing, he thinks
he can just drop by because it's his dog, and get this, he
thinks he's doing me a favor leaving the dog with me, so
I'll have some company since now I'm all *alone*. So one
day he comes over and I tell him the dog has run away,
but some people called and they have it, and here is the
number, and I give him the number of the vet, which of
course he doesn't recognize, since I was always the one
who took the fucking dog to the vet, right? So he calls,
and they tell him they've put the dog down like *his wife,
me*, told them to.'

The corners of her mouth are doing that wavery little

dance that precedes tears. For the passengers on the right side of the airplane we are passing Yosemite. She says, 'You probably think I'm terrible.'

'Not at all,' I say, and mean it. That's one thing about life in exville. The inhabitants are impressively tolerant. We're all heels, on some basic level. The same way Australia used to be full of prisoners, the land of exes is a land of people who make vows, then break them. So who am I to judge?

'When did he move out?' I'm imagining Adele's house, with the tragic pale squares on the wall where newly removed photographs used to hang; the garbage can brimming with old magazines and car manuals that he left behind, not to mention the now-useless dog bed.

'Nine years ago next month.'

I must have looked surprised. *Nine years* ago? As we banked for our final approach I thought it uncanny that Adele could still muster the energy to be enraged at a betrayal that took place so long ago.

'I know, I know. Why don't I get over it? Why *don't* I get over it?'

She pushed her bangs off her forehead with the back of her hand. She was sweating.

'I just read a book that said that 30 per cent of remarried men and 41 per cent of remarried women claim to be very angry, even ten years after their divorces,' I said. 'That's a pretty large percentage.'

'Huh. That does make me feel better. I'm not remarried. Do you think that means I'll be more angry, or angrier longer?'

The Internet provides a glimpse into the uncensored heart of the wounded ex-wife. One site features a message board devoted to revenge fantasies, with a box to check if the fantasy has been carried out. Angry exes order things off TV and send them to their former beloved, COD. One returned to the house she had shared with her ex and hid pieces of raw chicken under his mattress. Another put bleach in her husband's bottle of lubricating drops, which he used every morning prior to putting in his contact lenses. One woman destroyed her husband's seventy-thousand-dollar collection of vintage record albums. Another woman, an English Lady, capital 'L', cut off the cuffs of her husband's Saville Row suits and gave away his extremely expensive rare wine collection to street folk who normally enjoy their drinks from a paper bag. Another ex-wife sabotaged her ex-husband's wine collection by steaming all the labels off the bottles. (Note to graduate students: There's a thesis subject here – why do so many ex-husbands collect wine?)

Punctured tires. Smashed flowerpots. A garden hose turned on and fed into the basement window one weekend when the ex was out of town with his new girlfriend.

My favorite act of ex retribution is so inspired it should be reclassifed as performance art. Molly and Lawson lived in the country, on fifty-five acres he'd bought in the 1970s. Lawson, a jack-of-all trades, designed and built the house himself. As with most home renovation projects, money ran out at the end, and the upstairs bathroom was left unfinished. This wasn't too inconvenient, except in the middle of the night. It was a cold walk on wood floors from the master bedroom down the stairs and across the house to the downstairs bathroom. Lawson came up with an easier solution.

The bed Lawson shared with Molly, his wife of sixteen years, was set against a window, and it was simple for him to roll over and urinate out the window, into a part of the yard shrouded by a stand of Douglas fir. This soon became his regular habit, peeing out the master bedroom window onto the same patch of ground, night after night.

Soon, Lawson fell in love with a landscaper with whom he was working on a neighbor's retaining wall. He was happy to carry on an affair with the landscaper and did not particularly want to leave his marriage, or the house he'd built with his own hands on his fifty-five acres of land, but Molly was enraged. Molly nagged him. Molly wept. Molly threatened him. Finally, sadly, Lawson left.

Meanwhile, in the area by the side of the house where

he had been urinating for all those months, a patch of mushrooms grew. Oregon is famous for its wild mushrooms; I believe these were chanterelles, or some variety that would not look out of place in the average kitchen.

The day Lawson called to see if he might bring the divorce papers over to Molly to sign, she asked him to dinner. Relieved that Molly wasn't angry, Lawson happily accepted the invitation, and tucked into a steaming plate of rigatoni made with sausage and the chanterelles harvested from where they grew in abundance beneath his ex-bedroom window.

According to the United States Bureau of Justice, one third of all female murder victims are killed by an intimate. An 'intimate' is defined as a husband or ex-husband, a girlfriend or ex-girlfriend, a boyfriend or ex-boyfriend.

Only 4 per cent of male victims are killed by an intimate.

The number of men murdered by intimates has declined 60 per cent since 1976.

The number of women murdered by intimates has remained constant, with a slight dip occurring in 1993.

From these statistics we can surmise the following: When your husband or ex-husband, boyfriend or ex-boyfriend, says he's going to get you, pay attention.

Waste no time. Get out of the house, now. When your wife or ex-wife, girlfriend or ex-girlfriend, says she's going to get you, pay attention. Waste no time. Get your wine collection out of the house, now.

5

Appreciating the Beauty of
the Eternal Triangle

Where would we be without the love triangle? Some of the greatest books in history would never have been completed, published, or purchased for reprint by Penguin Classics. Imagine *Anna Karenina* without the sizzling affair between Anna and the dashing Count Vronsky. Instead of indulging her passion, Anna accepts her life with her cold-fish husband, the bureaucrat Alexey Karenin, and devotes herself to founding the Junior League, St. Petersburg branch. What would *Madame Bovary* be without Emma Bovary's self-administered cure for boredom, doomed intrigues with not one cad, but two? Consider: Emma is canny and practical (perhaps she is English instead of French), and rather than launching into her disastrous affair with the rich and cruel Boulanger, she realizes with the foresight of the sorority girl she would have been had she been born a hundred years later, that while hubby Charles may be a dud, at least he's a *doctor*. Instead of all that carrying on, she devotes her life to animal husbandry. And what about *The Great Gatsby*? It would have been *The So-So Gatsby* if the fabulously wealthy Jay Gatsby, rather than staging an entire life of extravagance for the benefit of Daisy Buchanan, did not spend most of his waking hours staring at the green light at the end of the dock, but instead ironed his collection of beautiful shirts.

Your triangle is probably a little less lofty and a lot more confusing than those mentioned above. For one thing, how can it be a triangle when no one's cheating? Anna was married to Karenin when she took up Vronsky, Emma was married to Bovary when she got the wandering eye, and Daisy was married to Tom Buchanan when she succumbed to Gatsby's ability to throw a great party.

But you're happily married, or happily cohabitating. All the drama and secret meetings and plate hurling is part of the increasingly distant past. If there was adultery going on before the marriage ended (although 70 per cent of those who divorce have a lover when the breakup occurs, only 15 per cent wind up marrying him or her), there isn't any going on now. Everyone is always in his or her appointed place.

Indeed, if you've come from a divorce anytime in the past ten years, you don't have *time* to cheat. Cheating takes time, and you get about four hours of sleep a night as it is. You're probably working like a ten-year-old in a Third World tennis shoe factory to pay your lawyer's bills (the student loans of Generation Ex); therapy bills; gym membership (the better to work off any untoward hostility that might manifest itself in doing something you might regret, like premeditated murder); 'maintenance' of the ex; child support if you're the noncustodial parent; or, if you're the custodial parent, the dozens of things child support doesn't begin to cover (presuming you're receiving any payments at all, despite the court order). There's also a chance you're angling to start a new second family, if you haven't already started one. I hear a good car seat costs about $130 these days. Ka-ching.

Your life, if it resembles anything vaguely theatrical, is the romantic comedy *One Fine Day*, the first movie whose theme is multitasking. George Clooney and Michelle Pfeiffer are Jake Taylor and Melanie Parker, each with an impossible, though attractive, ex-spouse, a successful New York career (he's a newspaper columnist, she's an architect), and a cutie-patootie in preschool. He has the Oedipally correct daughter; she has a son. They dash around Manhattan in the rain all day long (despite the opening scene, which shows Melanie late at night eating a slapped-together sandwich while paying bills at the coffee table, her divorce hasn't rendered her so destitute she was forced to move to Brooklyn), trading quips and trying to find adequate child care. The critics were universally unimpressed, failing to see that this bit of 'predictable fluff' (Roger Ebert) has more in common with one of Émile Zola's coal mine dramas than, say, *The Philadelphia Story*, which also featured exes who have nothing to do but trade witty banter. The most gratifying part is the end, when Jake and Melanie get together at her apartment, but fall asleep before they can get anything going sex-wise. A critic for salon.com pointed out that they're gorgeous and they just met; they can't, like, stay awake?

No. That's the point. It doesn't matter if you're gorgeous and relatively successful, as are Jack and Melanie (it's notable that only ten years ago, their respective careers of newspaper columnist and architect would have been portrayed as desirable, fast-track occupations; now they are merely middle-class). Unless you have round-the-clock help and a financial situation that allows you to live off the interest, at the end of the day, when you're an ex with a child and a job, you cannot stay awake. I hate to be the one to break the bad news.

In almost all ancient cultures, the triangle was the symbol of the female, and was revered in the same way Christianity reveres the cross. The triangle represented female genitalia. In tantric tradition it was the Triangle of Life, known as the Yoni Yantra, the sign of the vulva. In ancient Greece the triangle was delta, the symbol of Demeter, the mother of the harvest. The ancient Egyptian hieroglyphic for 'woman' is a triangle. Trotting out all these factoids based in prehistory is meant to lend weight to my observation that in the modern life of the ex, the eternal triangle (emphasis on the word 'eternal' − it seems as if it's never going to end, and there's a chance it won't) usually involves two women and a man.

The triangle that involves exes is a female construct from soup to nuts. While men happily involve themselves in extramarital liaisons (although the statistics vary, husbands do seem to cheat substantially more than do wives), once the marriage is dissolved and new teams are drafted (his wife is traded for his girlfriend, or his wife, who has left him, exercises her newly found free-agent status and signs with another team), *most* men (italics mine) figure out that there's nothing more for them to do, regardless of their feelings about the situation, and try to get on with their lives. Rarely are they the Other Man. Indeed, the Other Man as a concept almost doesn't exist. He's 'my lover', or 'someone else', as in, 'There's someone else.' People eager to gossip rarely ask, 'Who's the Other Man?' 'The Other Man' doesn't have the same connotation as 'The Other Woman'. 'The Other Man' sounds like an Alfred Hitchcock movie starring Orson Welles.

There are several basic triangles of exes.

a) Your husband, you, and the ex-wife, if you are the second wife.

b) Your ex-husband, you, and the second wife, if you are the ex-wife. You may think of yourself as 'the first wife' rather than 'the ex-wife'. That way you sound like a dynasty, and therefore deserve the sort of respect commonly accorded a Chinese empress.

c) Your husband, you, and the second ex-wife, if you are the third wife.

d) Your ex-husband, you, and the third wife, if you are the second ex-wife.

Note: In configurations c and d, if you are the first wife and are still lurking around your ex-husband's marriage, it's really time to find a new hobby, because that's what pining for him has become. There is nothing compelling about the eternal square, unless you're a lover of crossword puzzles.

How can you tell if you're in a triangle of exes?

Easy. The ex-wife thinks of reasons to call her ex-husband that would never have occurred to her while they were married, and it makes the current wife more furious than she's ever been in her entire life.

My friend Kiki happens to know Cindy, the new wife of Bernie, ex-husband of Leo, the well-spoken fundraiser with the hand towel problem from the Mae West Dinner

Party. Bernie, as you may recall, was the man who favored the pleasures of self-love rather than intercourse while he and Leo were allegedly trying to get pregnant. Leo left Bernie. Leo got the house and the better car. Bernie got the cat and a bleeding ulcer. But now, Leo misses Bernie. Leo, according to Cindy, Bernie's new wife, finds a reason to call at least once a day.

'She [Leo] leaves phone messages,' says Cindy, who is not a young trophy wife, but is the same age as Leo and is trying to establish herself as a graphic designer at age thirty-eight. 'She can't figure out how to turn up the temperature on the water heater. Or her wrist hurts, and she's worried it's a flare-up of her carpal tunnel problem. Doesn't Bernie remember her carpal tunnel problem? And how he used to massage her wrists with Tiger Balm, even though her doctor said it wouldn't do any good? The most recent is one of the best. The pilot light is out in the stove. She can't figure out what to do. This is a woman who played lacrosse in college and was an instructor for Outward Bound. Suddenly, she can't figure out about the pilot light? Even Donna Reed could figure out about the pilot light, for God's sake.'

Kiki and I were interested to hear this. One night, while our children were both at their fathers' houses, and we were sitting at the wooden kitchen table with our knees propped against the edge, drinking red wine and waiting for our chicken to bake, we got the idea to call Leo and ask her about this. We imagined that Cindy was being hypersensitive, that she was jealous of the history shared by Leo and Bernie, and that she was exaggerating. Or, we imagined that Leo, who is intelligent, accomplished, and possesses the usual self-awareness of an intelligent, accomplished, person who has been in some form of therapy since she could spell 'psychologist', would say, 'Aw, gosh, what can I say? Bernie may have had his bad points, but I miss him, and yes, I'm using these rather ridiculous ploys to get his attention.'

Leo answered the phone before the first ring. Not a good sign. She was obviously expecting Bernie, phoning back with advice on how to light the stove, recycle the newspapers, or put one foot in front of the other.

Kiki said, 'Leo, how's it going?' The only thing you ever need to say to an ex in the throes of a triangle.

Kiki heard about how Cindy refused to acknowledge that she, Leo, and Bernie had a shared past, and that even though they were no longer married, Bernie was still the one who knew the most about the peculiarities of the house that he'd dumped on her when he left. The house with the water heater that knocks and hisses whenever you touch it, and the porch with the dry rot – whatever the hell that is – and all of Leo's health problems, which Bernie was so good about advising her on. Better than her own damn doctor. 'I thought our big goal was always to be friends with our exes. So I'm trying to be civilized.

I'm trying to be friends. Why that bitch is so threatened is beyond me. I don't want him *back*. I'd just like a little help. Is that too much to ask? We were married, after all.'

For a month after the Underpants Episode, Claudia behaved like a nine-year-old girl angling for a pony. Children and employees desperate for a promotion are not the world's only suck-ups. An ex-spouse about to be permanently banished from a love triangle also needs to show that she is not as troublesome as she appears.

To get back in good with their exes, some ex-spouses might choose the less exhausting task of simply lying low. It works for bank robbers, and would work for exes as well, except doing nothing when there are so many statements to be made by one's actions is difficult indeed. Claudia's method of wooing Matthew was to demonstrate that she was no longer obsessed with him, and was busy making her new life. This was meant, I think, to get him to lower his guard.

In the seven days that followed the Episode, Claudia gave notice on her apartment in Portland and rented a house in a village that's a suburb of a suburb of Salem, Oregon's state capital, forty-six miles to the south. The village has a Quaker church, a post office, and a general store that rents videos and sells fishing licenses and dusty bags of pork rinds. Here, she planned to breed Nubian goats. As I mentioned before, Claudia is an epic animal lover, an animal lover in the way that we who think we are animal lovers – we let our dogs sleep with their heads on our pillows, staining our white pillowcases with their eye boogers – don't understand, an animal lover who has a need beyond the normal need for owning something cute and furry to chuck under the chin when she's feeling low. Indeed, whenever Claudia was depressed, instead of splurging on a pair of kicky sandals, she'd buy herself some livestock. She was anxious to assure Matthew that even though he, more than anyone else in her life, *knew* what animals meant to her, she was not just indulging herself. She was starting her own business. For she was going not only to breed Nubian goats, but also to produce goat cheese and goat milk, since all the Portland yuppies (including me, she hastened to add) love goat cheese and goat milk, and will pay a fortune for it. She bought six goats before she'd even signed the rental agreement at the new house. Pooh, Piglet, Roo, Kanga, Eeyore, and Tigger.

In the days before Claudia and Erica moved to the suburb of the suburb of Salem, Claudia ran errands for Matthew and brought him things she'd discovered while packing, important things from their marriage she thought he would want, such as one of those cardboard pine tree air fresheners that hang from a car's rearview mirror. At Matthew's suggestion, she made an appointment to get some counseling, then dutifully called him after both appointments to report on the progress she'd made, and to tell him how much better she was, and that, yes, yes, he was so right! Eeyore always knew just what was best for his Tigger! I say *both* appointments, because she was feeling so much better after the second one, she presumed she was cured of whatever problem it was that Matthew insisted she had.

Her phone calls continued at the same exhausting rate of one every ninety minutes or so, but she was always cheerful in the manner of a good-natured phone solicitor. Matthew managed the ongoing deluge of calls by ignoring them two thirds of the time. Eventually Claudia figured this out. How to circumvent this problem? Why, use the hostage, of course. Claudia's phone messages took on a new twist: Erica wanted to talk to her daddy. Erica, suddenly, always wanted to talk to her daddy. Erica, mysteriously, wanted to talk to her daddy about the same number of times a day that Claudia wanted to talk to her ex-husband. Urges to phone Daddy aside, however, Erica was deemed by Claudia too young to answer the phone. Matthew, torn, sensing a trap, would nevertheless return the call and get Claudia. If, during the phone call, Matthew displeased Claudia, she hung up, and Matthew would never get to speak to Erica at all. I wager this did relatively little damage to Erica, for the simple reason that most of the time Claudia invented Erica's urge as an excuse to call. Erica probably never even knew she was being enlisted.

Suddenly, in that one week, I'd had more exposure to Claudia than I'd had during the entire six months Matthew and I had been together. Prior to the Underpants Episode, he hadn't talked of her much. Like many good men, he was not eager to badmouth the mother of his child, or look stupid for having married her, or all the other reasons my friend Spud had suggested about why men are more close-mouthed about their exes than women are.

I couldn't escape feeling as if Claudia had become 'our' problem, mine and Matthew's. It was horrific, yet exciting, like battling a debilitating illness. We grew closer. We tried new restaurants, went dancing, made love as if we'd just met. We were united in some as-yet-undefined way against her. Matthew began asking my advice on how to handle her. Initially I was thrilled to be included in the fun. I didn't yet realize that 'handling' her implied that she would always be part of Matthew's life, and mine. I didn't know that a love triangle could also be a hate triangle.

On days I felt overwhelmed, I thought about Colette.

Sidonie Gabrielle Claudine Colette, French writer and aphorist (her most ex-applicable saying: 'You will do foolish things, but do them with enthusiasm') was married three times. Not only did she have ample experience being an ex, she also was in some of the literary world's weirdest triangles and quadrangles. Her separation and divorce from her first husband/collaborator/tormentor, Willy, was satisfyingly bizarre. Their marriage was unusual to begin with. A self-proclaimed writer, Henri Gauthier-Villars 'collaborated' with his young, provincial wife on several novels, which he then published under his penname, Willy. The four books, about a French provincial schoolgirl named Claudine, whose life mirrored Colette's almost exactly, made Willy famous.

This wasn't what got to Colette, however. What got to Colette was the usual thing. Colette left Willy because of his seemingly unquenchable passion for schoolgirls. French women are notoriously tolerant, and who knows whether it was the number of schoolgirls Willy took up with, or their characters, but the final straw was Willy's public infatuation with a rotund twenty-year-old chanteuse who took Willy's last name, Villars, as a stage name. Willy was hoping Colette would join him and Mademoiselle Villars, who insisted on calling Willy 'Papa', in a threesome. Colette stomped out, launched a notorious career in the theater (she specialized in playing roles that involved baring her breasts and passionately kissing women), and got involved with a rich transvestite who frequented Natalie Barney's infamous Parisian literary salon at 20 rue Jacob.

Colette's girlfriend, the Marquise de Belbeuf, or Missy, was an ideal ex, not once, but twice. Married at eighteen to the Marquis de Belbeuf, she divorced him without fuss several years later. Missy had cropped hair, a plain face, a barrel-shaped figure. She was frequently seen around Paris in tails, top hat, and gold monocle. Her true love was a girl who worked in a factory, with whom she'd had a brief fling. To commemorate this lost love, Missy would dress up as a factory worker herself, and spend hours in a special workroom making the kind of brass doorknobs made by the hands of the girl she'd once loved.

Now this is an achingly restrained and noble gesture. Missy was not harassing her ex-girlfriend with love letters, or showing up on the Parisian equivalent of the front lawn to declare herself at the top of her lungs. She was risqué, but not when it came to dealing with her pain. She suffered in silence, a fine old tradition that has gone the way of the pageant as a form of entertainment.

Colette and Willy were exes in the more modern style. Their first respective acts after breaking up were to flaunt their new, provocative associations: Colette moved in with Missy, and Meg Villars moved in with Papa Willy. During this time, Missy wrote a play about a scholar of ancient Egypt who falls in love with a mummy. Missy was to play the scholar, and Colette the mummy. The racy seduction scene involved the mummy stripping off her bandages in the kind of hubba-hubba dance that Ann-Margret would later make popular.

The play was held at the Moulin Rouge, home of the then-risqué French can-can, to a sold-out crowd. While Missy may have been an exemplary ex, her ex-husband, the Marquis de Belbeuf, was not. His concern was not that his ex-wife had turned out to be a doorknob-crafting Sapphist, but that she would dare to drag the Belbeuf name through the mud by writing and starring in such a scandalous production. His revenge was to pack the house with friends and family. The instant the curtain went up, he and his supporters began throwing chairs, eyeglass cases, hats, even heads of garlic (meant to convey that this, literally, stinks) at his ex-wife.

Meanwhile, Willy and Meg Villars were sitting near the stage in a box seat. After the mummy striptease, there was a lingering kiss between the mummy and the scholar, and Willy began whistling and applauding, stamping his feet, mocking the performers. This had the unhappy result of drawing attention to himself and Meg, and when the audience realized that here was the husband who could not control his wife, who in fact condoned her behavior by showing up at her raunchy performances with his own lover, there was a stampede. He tried to beat off his persecutors with his cane, but the police had to come and escort him out of the theater.

Even after Willy filed for a legal separation from Colette

on the grounds that she had deprived him of his conjugal rights by leaving him, and she countered with a suit that listed his blatant adulteries, Colette wanted Willy back. While they were waiting for the final paperwork, Colette was still writing letters to Willy, pleading for a reconciliation. Her pleadings were either classic or cliché, depending on your point of view: 'Without you, I'm nothing.' Still, she refused to give up Missy, and Willy refused to give up Meg. They were at an impasse, until Willy sold the rights to the Claudine books without consulting Colette, for a price that amounted to giving them away. The split was final in 1909; she went on to live forever in the minds and on the T-shirts and canvas book bags of eager American undergraduates and public television subscribers, and he died poor, known only for locking his ex-wife in a room and making her write.

6

The Language of Things

I fear I've given the impression that the life of the ex
is nothing but one confounding, frustrating escapade
after the next. That the personal motto of every ex is,
'What fresh Hell is this?' There are happy exes, people
who, for reasons having to do with temperament, luck,
and relative financial security, get along with all the
ex-spouses, current wives and husbands, half-children
and step-children as if they were nothing more than a
large family of loosely associated cousins.

A marriage counselor offered to put me in touch with
Lucinda, a former client whom the counselor felt had
managed to avoid a lot of the pitfalls of living in exville.
Lucinda was a massage therapist and had had an affair with
one of her clients. It went on for six months, but Lucinda
was too consumed with guilt to have the fun she thought
she was supposed to be having. 'The sex was worse with

my lover than with my husband, because I was so nervous all the time.' She ended the affair, but not before her husband, Michael, found out (the usual: suspicious credit card bills) and used his anger at her betrayal as a lever out of the marriage. Michael was a chiropractor and left Lucinda for one of *his* clients. Michael and Lucinda have one daughter, Hailey, and Michael has a daughter and infant with his new wife, to whom he's been married for five and a half years.

When I spoke to Lucinda on the phone, she said her secret for getting along with her ex and her ex's new wife was simple: an unwavering commitment to the path of nonattachment. 'I don't think about the stuff,' she said. She had the kind of low, tranquilizing voice I always imagined would belong to a female hypnotist.

For our interview, I asked to meet Lucinda at her house; I wanted to see how the path of nonattachment translated into real-life decorating challenges. I expected something in the Shaker tradition: white walls, pine floors buffed to an elegant sheen, a small, Mission-style sofa. Spare, tasteful, beautifully monastic. Truthfully, I expected to dislike Lucinda, to find her smug, to listen to some Buddhist manifesto, then find out from my marriage counselor friend that while Lucinda allowed Michael to have every last bit of overmicrowaved Tupperware in the house, she also had a fat trust fund.

Lucinda lived two streets over from a street of million-dollar homes in northeast Portland. Two streets over, it cost somewhere in the low five figures to reroof the house, and hundreds per month to heat it in the winter. Two streets over, every house employed three gardeners, one for the lawn, one for the flower beds, and an arborist for the trees. Lucinda's house was a tract house with red vinyl siding built on a spare lot sometime during the 1970s, plunked down amid modest, but pretty, craftsman bungalows, with their low-slung roofs and huge, inviting porches. It was surrounded by a low chain link fence.

Inside was brown sculpted hi-lo shag carpeting and a purple velour sofa that was missing its little legs. The textured walls were dirty bone white and bereft of the paintings I'd supplied for them in my imagination (I'd envisioned Lucinda a water colorist who framed her own). The focal point of the living room was the televisions, stacked one atop the other. Lucinda explained that the sound worked on one, and the picture worked on the other, so they had to have them both on at the same time. Across from the TV were a pair of patio chairs, the kind with the vinyl straps that leave cruel-looking lines pressed into the backs of your thighs. What broke my heart: one was adult size, with blue and green straps, and the other was a matching child's size. This is where Lucinda and her daughter, Hailey, watched PBS together. The place smelled like old cooking oil.

Lucinda was small, with what people used to call the wiry build of a ten-year-old boy, but ten-year-old boys can be enormous these days. She reminded me of one of those magical creatures who lived in the forest, with her short auburn hair and slanted eyes. We sat at either end of the purple velour sofa. She didn't offer me anything to drink.

'It seemed less painful simply to let Michael have it all than having to go over who gets the wok and who gets the alarm clock. It was already an awful situation. Why make it worse? Why spend time and emotional energy arguing over, say, the sofa – this is a St. Vincent de Paul special, and you can see it's perfectly good – when what we'd really be hollering about is how I stepped out on him and he stepped out on me and how did it all end up so badly. Because that's what people are really fighting about when they're fighting about the stuff.

'And in case you start feeling sorry for me – I know this place looks like the communal living room of Teen Challenge, by the way – think of it this way: Michael got the house, sure, but Michael also got twenty years' worth of junk I didn't want to think about, including a closet full of old clothes. Let's see, there's a few very expensive, butt-ugly bridesmaid's dresses that now belong to Michael. A hot pink linen jacket that looked like Rod Stewart during his comeback years, also Michael's. Two decades of coffee-stained bathrobes, those are lovely. About ten years' worth of Christmas sweaters, the kind with felt appliqués. I don't feel so bad that Michael got those; his mother has matching ones.' Lucinda cracked herself up, thinking about that closet full of clothes. She bent over and screeched. I was transfixed. A laughing ex-wife. I noted this was the same sartorial detritus Claudia had kept in Matthew's closet, only in her case they were old clothes masquerading as one more tentacle wrapped around the rock of the old marriage.

'. . . The point is, what am I going to do, make Michael's life miserable – and mine, too, by the way – by making the stuff a battleground? Just because the marriage didn't last? People have always been forced to start over, for a variety of reasons. My mother lost half her family in the San Francisco earthquake of 1905 – *and* their house. I have friends who lost everything in the Northridge earthquake of 1989. In any case, I appreciate what I have now. I'm saving up to buy a dining room table, just like people used to do in the old days, before we all started living on credit. I'm looking forward to shopping for it and purchasing it and having the delivery guys deliver it. Sometimes I think about the day I'm finally able to buy it as a way of helping myself go to sleep at night. It's that nice.'

I'm impressed. I tell her she seems to have a handle on this.

'I didn't say it was easy,' she says. Suddenly, she isn't laughing any more.

For centuries people communicated in the language of flowers. The gift of a pink rose meant friendship and endearment, while a white rose meant 'I am worthy of you.' A yellow rose meant jealousy. Any type of red flower – a tulip, rose, carnation, or chrysanthemum – was a declaration of love. It wasn't simply romantic news that was conveyed through flowers. A posy could communicate a threat, or even a request for money. Give someone a sprig of basil and you were telling him you despised him. You'd better hope he's a horticultural whiz kid, because sweet basil meant good luck. One presumes that a nice mixed bouquet of standard basil and sweet basil meant 'get lost and good luck.'

Exes speak the language of things. During the divorce, every side table and coat hook, every last toothbrush cup and paper towel rack, becomes a bearer of subtext, a tool for retaliation, or an olive branch. One guilty ex leaving a marriage may give his soon-to-be-ex-wife the entire house and everything in it as a way of assuaging his guilt (his lawyer will advise against it). Another ex, enraged at being left, is determined not to be awarded the things she loves in the house, but the things *he* loves. She wants the big-screen TV, the Soloflex machine, and the vintage TR7.

To learn the language of things, tune in to *Divorce Court* any day of the week, and there you'll see people on the verge of heart failure, spittle gathered in the corners of their mouths, fighting over who gets the Crock Pot. On a recent episode, the divorcing couple spent their entire fifteen minutes of fame bickering over the sound systems. The soon-to-be-ex-husband was in the nightclub business, and as a result had nine sound systems of varying size and quality. The main bone of contention was that he was going to be awarded five of them, and she only four, even though she lived in an apartment and already had one, a gift from her new boyfriend, also in the nightclub business.

The unfortunate part of this is that for many exes, it really is about a sofa. The average price of a good sofa is easily over a thousand dollars. A living room can exist without a coffee table. It can exist without rugs. You don't need lamps, because there's always the overhead. Without a sofa, however, you're looking at a couple of folding chairs, you're looking at an AA meeting, a group therapy session, the lobby of the Salvation Army: a living room where no one wants to live, a place that advertises how badly things are going. Sometimes one spouse really does need the sofa, and it's terrible if the other one winds up with it.

There are loads of stories about how people split up their possessions when they divorce. Sitcoms have done to death the divorcing couple who engage in endless, life-sucking skirmishes about who gets custody of the dachshund and who gets the cell phone. Few people think about the fate of the stuff after it becomes the property of one of the exes.

After everything is split up, and safely settled in its new spot on the mantel or in the far corner of the basement, it takes on a weird life of its own. The hideous gold and orange ceramic lamp that, during the marriage, should have been in the living room but wound up for some reason in the bedroom, becomes an emblem of some part of the failed marriage. It becomes that hideous lamp he insisted on keeping because he had it in his first apartment – the apartment he had when you dated! The apartment where you first made love! – which you despised, but you gave in, because that's how it *always* was. You giving in. Even though the lamp was far too big for the night table, even though it looked so stupid there. Whatever minimal neutrality the lamp possessed during the marriage mysteriously vanishes.

Then, after the divorce has receded somewhat into the past, another transformation occurs. Let's say you got the sofa. It sits there reminding you of the marriage for months or years. Then, after you've wept alone with your face mashed into the cushions, and smooched there with a few disastrous dates, and spilled a glass of wine from a party you hosted without the ex, you realize it now has an associative life beyond the marriage. It has grown, in a sense, just as you have. Still, a film of memories stubbornly adheres to it, the way the drizzle of volcanic ash from Mount St. Helens's eruption settled on the trees of the Pacific Northwest and despite nearly three decades of rain, still coats the branches of the highest boughs.

You fall in love with someone else, finally, and here is the sofa, staring the both of you in the face. Accusingly, your new love may think. The sofa from the old marriage. The sofa with suspicious stains.

A friend from film school, a film editor named Clara, had a peculiar experience with her ex possessions. Rob, her ex, made an independent feature for about ten dollars and used a lot of the things from their house as props. Their entire house, more or less as it was when she and Rob were married, was one of the movie's main sets. There it was, on the big screen, the big book-case she'd painted the color of tired lox. The stunted ficus that failed either to die or thrive. The pictures of old friends and family in the background, *her* family. There were all the books she'd left, the rows of Vintage Contemporaries from the 1980s, with their colorful spines, the entire set of Will and Ariel Durant's Civilization series she'd gotten for free when she joined the Book-of-the-Month Club sometime in the late 1970s, with the idea of becoming a great intellectual, the entire panorama of western civilization at her fingertips. 'I think the only time I ever took them out of the bookcase was to flatten the corners of a rolled-up poster,' she told me.

The most poignant things left over from a marriage are the rings. What to do with those? They're probably some of the few things that are genuinely worth something outside of the garage sale market. I took an informal poll. Kiki had picked out her own wedding ring, diamonds and sapphires set in an antique yellow gold setting; she still wears it on her wedding-ring finger.

Another friend, with two marriages behind her, hawked the first engagement ring, a diamond solitaire, at a pawn shop on Manhattan's 42nd Street. 'I was twenty-six years old, strutting down Forty-Second with twenty-six hundred in my pocket. I haven't felt so rich since.' Her second engagement ring was a family heirloom that belonged to her ex-husband's grandmother. That one she returned.

My first wedding ring is in a tin candy box covered with pink roses, where I keep my earrings and cheap bracelets. I must be trying to pretend it's just another piece of jewelry. My ex-husband didn't wear a wedding ring. Matthew's wedding ring is rattling around the glove compartment of his truck. His idea was to pawn it, but he can't quite bring himself to do it.

Many exes choose the pawn shop route. Vincent, the

guy who works the counter at a pawn shop downtown, says, 'People who wouldn't normally come in here for anything else come to pawn their rings. I can see 'em coming. They take anything I offer. They're just happy to have that part over with, I guess.'

You'd be surprised how many exes choose burial at sea.

My favorite story is about Elise, a woman who knew the pastry chef baking the cake for her ex-husband's second wedding. Several days before the wedding she invited herself to the pastry chef's kitchen, and when no one was looking, dropped her wedding band into the cake mold holding the batter for the top tier of the cake, the one traditionally frozen and saved for the first wedding anniversary. Elise couldn't wait for the day, a year's hence, when her ex or his second wife chipped a tooth on her platinum band.

Claudia was particularly sensitive to the power and the aura of belongings. She herself could not bear the thought that Matthew had lived with someone before he met her. When Claudia moved into the condo Matthew had shared with his ex-girlfriend, she made him throw out all the sheets, blankets, and pillows, as well as an entire set of dishes.

It makes sense, the way it makes sense when a first-grade boy is concerned about getting cooties from a first-grade girl, but not when you price out a complete set of linens for a queen-sized bed.

After Claudia moved to the suburb of the suburb of Salem with her goats, she started sending Matthew big care packages, the kind a mother traditionally sends to a son in the Peace Corps. Flannel shirts, malted milk balls, Rain-X for the windshield of his car, Winnie-the-Pooh boxers. Homemade fudge. Books she thought he'd like. Matthew, unable to ask her to stop, eventually began dropping the boxes in the trash can as soon as they arrived.

7

The Art of Abusing the Telephone

In Edwardian England the home headed up by an ex-wife was described by frowning sociologists as 'a pandemonium of domestic misery'. This is an accurate description of the Kate and Allie House after Matthew and Erica moved in.

This was such a bad decision, it deserves a little ink. The house Matthew rented with the bicycle delivery guys had been sold out from under them by the landlord. Matthew decided to buy a house. He had to be out in thirty days, but even if he found something he wanted to buy in that length of time, he wouldn't have time to close on the deal. He laid this out for me one night at a local brew pub where we used to go for their throw-pillow-sized pieces of pizza. As he was talking, I yelled inside my head, DO NOT ASK HIM TO MOVE IN! DO NOT ASK HIM TO MOVE IN!

'Well honey, you could always stay with me and Kiki until you found something.'

'I'd be looking for a place big enough for all of us, you know.' He covered my hand with his own. He was good.

Why I did this, I don't know. Perhaps I was afraid he would move in with Claudia. Perhaps I was rebelling against a lifetime of always feeling like the designated driver, even when no one was drinking. Perhaps I was unconsciously identifying with and competing with Claudia, like in an Ingmar Bergman movie. She had a screwed-up life; I wanted one too. Matthew moved in two weeks later.

More times than I care to remember, it was three adults (me, Kiki, Matthew) and three children (Katherine, Philly, Erica), two bedrooms, and one bath, an arrangement that reminded Kiki of the big rundown houses with lots of people she lived in during her hippie youth, and me of those independently made Irish movies that American critics and audiences eat up – so warm, so beguiling, so human – never seeing that they are extolling a way of life that includes seventeen people sharing a single bathroom.

Before Matthew moved in I had arranged my room just how I'd wanted it. The freedom to make autonomous decorating decisions is one of the few benefits of divorce. During the first months after I'd moved in with Kiki, I would sit propped up on my pillows (which were the perfect, cheap foam flatness I required) and gaze at the teetering, too-tall bookcase holding just two shelves of books I loved (not one so-so paperback in the bunch, stuck in there simply because I couldn't figure out what else to do with it), the old dresser Kiki and I found at a secondhand shop, with three drawers, white porcelain knobs, a large unreliable mirror attached with a wooden frame, and on the dresser a picture of Katherine vamping during her swimming lessons in a purple flowered bathing suit, and a picture of me in my scuba gear sitting on the gunwale of a dive boat off the coast of Puerto Rico. There was not one thing in this room that I hadn't chosen, that I didn't like. I consoled myself for my divorce with this thought more times than I can count.

Then Matthew moved in with his few things (he'd gotten rid of the huge useless cabinet), colonized one of the closets, bought a television and a computer. An entire household full of activity went on in my – now our – room. In the evenings I would read on the bed while Matthew wrote his lesson plans on the computer, or I would write on the computer while Matthew flopped on the bed and watched a video. I made too many tasteless jokes about Anne Frank. I had dreams about living on a submarine.

The kids' room, the one painted a demented aqua, was right next door. The three kids shared the two bunks, reminding me of 'hot bunks', as they are known on the tiny Pacific island of Ebeye, part of the Marshall Island chain. Ebeye is the most densely populated island on earth. Fifteen thousand people live on seventy-eight acres, and few families have enough beds, so they trade off. The children sleep at night while the parents, most of whom are unemployed, wander around, and the parents sleep during the day when the children are in school. Since all of us had joint custody with our respective exes, we tried to have one child with the other parent at any given time, in order to have beds for the two who were here. On days when we were unable to execute the necessary scheduling gymnastics, we had all the kids at once and they drew straws to see who would sleep on the sofa with Mabel the Bad Breath Dog.

To cut down on the domestic pandemonium it was decided that Matthew should have his own telephone line. The Red Phone, as it came to be known, wasn't for Matthew, of course. It was for Claudia.

There are exes all over the world (in the history of civilization only the Incas and the Roman Catholic Church expressedly forbade divorce), but there are none so unhappy as those in Western cultures, and I lay the blame squarely at the foot of Alexander Graham Bell. As part of the divorce decree, exes should agree to communicate only by written letter, sent by regular mail. It would save everyone a lot of Rolaids, glimpses into their secret murderous natures, and give the postal service a shot in the arm as well.

The average !Kung bushman of the Kalahari Desert may have five or six spouses in a lifetime. The Yoruba of West Africa dissolve their marriages at least as often as we do in the West do (their divorce rate is 46 per cent). The Hadza, who live around the Olduvai Gorge, have a divorce rate five times higher than that of the United States.

What I find amazing here is not that men and women in so-called primitive societies can't make it work; but that their post-divorce lives are relatively stress free. A !Kung couple may scream and yell, weep and throw rocks and baobab fruit rinds at each other for months before they split up, but when they split up, they split up. One of them gathers together his or her things and leaves the tribelike group of ten or so families that lives around a particular source of water, and moves on to another water source, where he or she is accepted into another community of far-flung kin. The children stay, or the children go.

In any case, there are no electronic leashes slung on the short animal-skin aprons worn by !Kung men. No answering machines, voice messaging services, call-forwarding, call-waiting, e-mail, fax machines, portable phones, or cell phones. There is no easy opportunity to pester, harass, browbeat, bully, bait, or hound. If a !Kung ex-wife wants to tell a !Kung ex-husband that he is an insufferable sack of shit and she doesn't know what she was thinking when she ever agreed to forage for him – and does he remember how she used to go out of her way to find him those special mongongo nuts that he just had to have, and would any of his other wives ever bring him those stupid nuts the way she did?, she even polished the shells, for God's sake! — she has to walk dozens of miles in the blistering desert heat to the water hole where he may or may not still be living. Needless to say, it's not worth it.

The exes of the West insist on regarding the telephone as a convenience, except, I imagine, Mr Fukumoto of Kawasaki, Japan. His ex-wife, a certain loquacious Naoya Fukumoto, was finally arrested by police for having made over a hundred thousand crank phone calls to her ex-husband over the span of two years. Her monthly phone bill was half her salary. Her personal best was 200 calls in one day. (I was lucky; the most calls Claudia ever made in one day was 43.) On the day the police entered Ms Fukumoto's apartment to arrest her, she was, of course, on the phone to her ex-husband. Her last words to him as she rang off were, 'You idiot!'

I bet, without knowing for sure, that Ms Fukumoto didn't simply call Mr Fukumoto to rant like a lunatic. Why would Mr Fukumoto have put up with it for two full years? Because her phone calls were not unvarnished harassment, but harassment disguised as concern, as a question, as a mere conveying of information. I'm sure, like many exes, men and women included, she came up with an excuse to call.

There are an unlimited number of excuses to call when you've been married to someone. The *M'Aidez* Call is the call for help. Usually the *M'Aidez* Call is a plea for money. There are so many unforeseeable monetary circumstances when one is an ex, financial snafus that only your ex can remedy. Floating a small loan from a buddy at work for your child's Easter basket and the attendant chocolate bunnies, jelly beans, and speckled malted-milk-ball eggs, is unthinkable. Yet phoning up your ex and begging for thirty bucks to be able to play the Easter Bunny is certainly within the realm of reason. (I can be fairly sure that Ms Fukumoto was not phoning Mr Fukumoto for money to buy a box of Marshmallow Peeps, but you get the drift).

A second variation on the *M'Aidez* Call is a call for assistance. This is the plea made by the ex-wife for help in talking to the mechanic who purposely misdiagnosed the engine knock in the car you once shared. I'm not being sexist, merely ex-ist; no ex-husband, however desperate, would ask his ex-wife to intercede on his behalf in the automotive realm. This is not the case with, say, their mutual hairstylist. One ex-husband I know used to call his ex-wife at work every time he went in for a haircut, cajoling the ex-wife into calling Brianna to ask her to do that thing she did that one time to give him more volume on the top.

The Venting Phone Call is a special favorite of exes who have torturous, complicated relationships with family members that only the ex can appreciate, having suffered through them him- or herself for years. Claudia called countless times when she'd had a fight with her mother; she also called when she anticipated an argument, at which time the phone call neatly dovetailed into the Advice Phone Call. You know my mother; how should I handle her?

The Advice Phone Call should not be confused with the *M'Aidez* Phone Call, Assistance Division. The Advice Phone Call is protean, multipurpose. All you are asking the ex to do is listen. Another of Claudia's favorites was the New Vehicle Inquiry Call. I can say with confidence that no one save the purchasing agent of Hertz International ever entertained the notion of buying a new car more often than Claudia. Not that she had in recent history purchased a new car. The genius of this type of phone call is that there isn't a time of the day or night when one might not be contemplating getting a new car, and when this happens, one certainly needs the advice of someone who knows something about cars.

The Shoulder-to-Cry-On Call is the one where the

ex has had a bad day at work, or an argument with her mother, and simply needs to talk. This is even more versatile than the Advice Call, because her ex-husband isn't even required to appear to be listening.

In the end, these excuses will not yield the response the Naoya Fukumotos of the world truly seek. For the *M'Aidez* Call, the Advice Call, the Venting Call, the Shoulder-to-Cry-On Call rarely promote the necessary degree of attachment the ex desires. Setting aside for a moment the joy of soaking the ex for some cash, you don't really want the ex's help, advice, shoulder, or ear; you want to kill him, or you want him back, and pumping him about the advantages of antilock brakes versus whatever the other option is won't get you closer to either of those goals.

The Going Mental Phone Call never fails to elicit some response, even if it's a click in your ear. The Going Mental Call, Fuck You Division, is where the ex who did not initiate the divorce calls and cusses out the ex-spouse for ruining his or her life. The Going Mental Call, Fuck Me Division, is where the ex calls weeping because he realizes that he was such a loser, he drove her away.

Claudia is a master of phone manipulation. She was indefatigable, proving she'd missed her calling in life as Employee of the Month at a successful collection agency. She could think of a galaxy of reasons to call, then expertly transform a harmless Advice Phone Call into a Venting Phone Call into a Shoulder-to-Cry-On Phone Call. Wow.

More impressively, she could start the phone call as a Going Mental Call, mold it within moments into an Advice Phone Call, segueing into the New Vehicle Inquiry Call.

'I hate you, sob sob, if you didn't leave me I wouldn't have to deal with this stupid car, sob sob, the window knob handle thingy fell off the door; how am I supposed to get the window up? Maybe I should just get a new one. Car, not window thingy. Do you know anything about those new Saturns?'

One call was seldom enough to accomplish whatever goal Claudia had drummed up as a reason to call in the first place. Follow-up phone calls in both the nondementia and Going Mental categories displayed her true gift for harassment. Did you say you were going to put the money into my account this morning or this afternoon? Is it a V-6 or a V-8? Nine-thirty or 10:30? Tomato or Tomahto? If the call suddenly, unexpectedly or by design, morphed into one of the Going Mental Calls, either variety, she slammed the phone down mid-conversation, then immediately called back either to tell Matthew never to call her again or to announce she was leaving the country with Erica and he would never speak to his daughter again.

The most successful type of phone call, and the one I

imagine Ms Fukumoto used masterfully (200 phone calls a day, come on) is the Search for Pity Phone Call.

Imagine you are Matthew. It's 10:30, 11:30 at night. Not tragedy-late, but late enough for the caller to get her sad-sack point across. It's not so late you'd let the machine pick up. It's not, say, 2:30, just after the bars close. It's not 5:00 A.M. when someone might be calling from another time zone with news of a death.

It's Claudia, of course, calling from a pay phone near a freeway, traffic rumbling past in the background. Her phone has been disconnected for nonpayment, the second time in six months. Every minute or so you hear the cling-cling of the quarters. She has been weeping, but is now subdued. Erica is sleeping in the car, Claudia says, beginning to cry again. She's exhausted. Tomorrow, Claudia will search through the bottom of her purse, and under the seat of her car (the window still won't roll up), and see if she can scrape together enough change to buy a gallon of gas to get Erica to school. She knows she shouldn't have quit her job, but she just hated it so much. What's wrong with her, that she has such bad luck? That she drove such a good, kind, sexy, supportive man like you away? That her life is so awful and miserable?

Claudia liked to call first thing in the morning, seven days a week, and as many times as it suited her until midnight, and sometimes after, depending on whether or not it had been a tough day. To his credit, Matthew did not always answer the phone. But he ignored her calls at his own peril. For if she was unable to talk to him, she would start getting desperate and the messages would pile up on the answering machine, ten, twelve, twenty. Day after day after day.

Thus Pavlov's theory was proven once again. When Claudia was really blazing she would call first the Red Phone, then the house phone, then the Red Phone, then the house phone, until she finally provoked somebody into responding. After a few weeks of this, every time the phone would ring, my stomach felt as if strong hands inside me were trying to strangle it. A hysterical voice in my head would shriek: Now what? Now what? Now what? Once, when Matthew and I were at the movies and I was waiting for him outside the men's room, a nearby pay phone started to ring, and my hands started shaking.

I thought: It's Claudia calling to say she won't be able to go to work today because she doesn't have any money for gas (the general subject of a phone call one Monday morning at 6:30), or that she's quit her job (Friday before a long weekend; about 7:00 P.M.), or she has an interview today for a job that pays seven cents more an hour, but has no money for panty hose (weekday, 11:30 A.M.), or that her car's been broken into and her radio stolen (one Sunday at 7:15 A.M.), or she's had an argument with her mother and is going to be forced to sleep in her car (same Sunday, 10:30 P.M.). She quit her job (Monday after a long weekend). She hates her life so much, she threw up in her night class (Thursday, 8:30 P.M.). She has gone to see a counselor like Matthew told her to, but the Zoloft she's on now makes her constipated (forget which day, 1:30 A.M.). If it wasn't for Erica, she would jump off a bridge (Friday, 5:45 P.M., 6:30 P.M., 6:40 P.M., 6:45 P.M., 6:47 P.M.) Could Matthew please call and advise her about a car she's thinking of buying? (Same Friday, 7:30 P.M.)

I am a woman who prays, not well, and not often, but not only when I'm flying through turbulence. I thank God for my health. I thank God for my child and her health. I thank God that when Claudia was in her most ferociously communicative phase cell phone technology was still in its infancy. I prayed for her eradication from planet earth. If it could happen to smallpox, why couldn't it happen to Claudia?

8

Talk Medea to Me

I find it hard to believe that the life of the child of divorce – a tragedy of which most exes with children are acutely aware – is categorically worse than a lot of the questionable experiences kids have always endured at the hands of adults. There have been no real golden ages for children, setting aside the lives of all the children on the island nation of Bali – where babies are revered by all citizens, each one passed around like a just-opened present, their feet never allowed to touch the ground until they're something like seven – and all twelve-year-old monarchs throughout the ages. Unless you were born Balinese or a pharaoh, being a kid on planet earth isn't, and has never been, a load of laughs.

Until about eighty years ago, if a kid dodged mumps, measles, diphtheria, and polio (conscientious mothers now feel guilty getting their children inoculated for these nasty diseases – 'I'm injecting my baby with toxins!'), chances were he'd be forced to do the kind of work that inspired the creation of labor unions. Dropped down into coal mines, marched off to sweatshops, ordered into the fields. In school, if he was fortunate enough to go to school, he'd be smacked with a ruler for fiddling around in his desk when he was supposed to be memorizing *The Rime of the Ancient Mariner*. At the end of the day, he'd be given broth but no chicken, because that was reserved for the man of the family. He shared a bedroom, maybe a bed, probably with more than one person.

It was not uncommon for men whose wives had died to simply take their children over to some female relative, drop them off, and never return. Junior: 'When's Father coming back?' Auntie: 'Never. You were too much for him to handle.' Now there's a parent who had no fear of saddling his child with abandonment issues.

You can't tell me that the struggles of a more or less beloved child of joint custody, who spends, say, one week at Mom's and one week at Dad's, and at each place has a fully furnished room of his own, each with its own bookcase, toy box, stuffed animal collection that needs thinning, closet full of clothes – there's probably a PlayStation or a Game Boy tossed in there, too – has it worse than my Great Aunt Maude, who, at age six, was locked in the outhouse when she failed to scrub the floor to her mother's specifications, a job she was required to perform every night after dinner. She was in there an hour for each spot she missed. The child whose parents are divorced certainly experiences a more poignant existence, but the mere fact of being the child of exes doesn't make it tragic.

When my ex-husband and I divorced we did it ourselves, with the help of a mutual attorney friend. There's a small stationery store downtown, across the street from the courthouse, that sells only legal forms. There are several different forms to file for divorce in the state of Oregon, and while I was standing in the aisle trying to figure out which ones I needed, a voice from behind me said, 'Have you given thought to your children?'

An older woman, on the other side of the aisle, looking for who knows what forms. She had extremely shiny black shoes, an expensive wool coat, the kind of blue eyes that lose their color with age, gloves. It took me a minute to realize she'd been reading over my shoulder. She nodded pointedly at the forms in my hand.

There have been a spate of well-publicized studies showing that women experience a drop in self-esteem after having read a fashion magazine (how they measure this, I can't imagine), but you never hear about how sitcoms damage the self-image of people who like to think they're good with a comeback. All those withering retorts, those snappy one-liners. Normally, I would answer someone like this truthfully, politely without even thinking, then curse myself ten minutes later for not having given her the finger. But that day, for some reason, I was feeling puckish.

Instead I said, '*Who?* Oh, them.'

Do people who disapprove of divorce for couples with children really imagine we don't consider our kids? That we don't suffer insomnia over this lifelong wound we're aware we've inflicted? That we don't chew our cuticles, scanning the landscape of our children's lives constantly for trouble on the horizon? There is never a week when my ex and I make the kid exchange that I don't get a twinge of sorrow to hear Katherine, the first day in my house, trying to get herself reacclimated, flipping aloud through her mental Rolodex of names: 'Daddy – Gramma – Mrs Albert (her teacher) – *Mom*, can I have a peanut butter and jelly sandwich?'

I'm not saying all this so you'll think I'm an exemplary mother, just so you'll realize that, yes, I have given a thought to my child. Whereas I don't think my father-in-law's father lost a wink of sleep over beating his boy because he was struggling to read. He was a married man, a good provider, a strict father (strict fathering, in those days, equaling good fathering), so his behavior was unimpeachable according to the standards of society. I'm sure he slept the hard, dreamless sleep of the righteous.

If anything, contemporary exes think about their kids *too* much. We overparent to overcompensate for the divorce. We do the math all wrong. We figure: My child may not have a live-in father, but he does have Tae Kwon Do, Suzuki violin lessons, math and art enrichment courses, and as much face time with me as his heart desires. Exes, who don't have the luxury of having their kids underfoot all the time, are loathe to say, 'I'm reading right now, go play' (to the child's detriment, I might add).

I was at my friend Leslie's house. Leslie's ex situation, in brief: Rocky, her college-sweetheart husband, fooled around with his company's attorney; Leslie tossed Rocky out and filed for divorce the same week; soon-to-be ex-husband Rocky and lawyer-sweetie split; by then Leslie was temporarily engaged to someone else, but had a brief fling with Rocky, now her official ex, while fiancé was rock-climbing in Indonesia; nevertheless, she decided it was really really over with Rocky; fiancé returned, and she decided it was really really over with him, too, since otherwise, why would she have been tempted to sleep with her ex? One child: Benny, who is allergic to dairy, obsessed with reptiles, and enjoys working the word 'carnage' into every conversation.

Benny came in one day while Leslie and I were sitting at her kitchen table drinking tea, and asked if they could go camping, just Leslie and him. Leslie's face melted into an expression of sadness last seen on a street mime. She said, 'Gosh, Benny Bunny, I understand your desire to go camping, but it's just not good for me right now. I promise I'll think about it and we'll see what we can do. This isn't a promise, but I am taking your request very seriously, all right? Because what you want is important to me, okay?'

Benny pitched a moderate fit, and was happy to go off with a juice box and a bowl of Cheez Puffs.

One day, when I was a little older than Benny, I went into the kitchen while my mother was sitting at our Formica breakfast bar drinking her beer, smoking her cigarette, and making a shopping list on a steno pad, and asked the same question Benny did. 'Mom, can we go camping sometime?'

She laughed, cocked her face up at the ceiling, blew a few smoke rings, and said, 'Over my dead body.' My mother, safe within her rock-solid middle-class marriage, had the luxury of allowing me to be unhappy.

Thus the rooms jam-packed with toys, the lessons, the play dates, the hand-wringing concern every time an ex's daughter is sad, or an ex's son brings home a note from school about how he's been shoving in line. The line-shover of an intact family is simply being a kid; the line-shover raised by exes, either one or both, is very possibly screwed up because of the divorce. Truth be told, we expect the kids of divorce to have problems. Witness how surprised everyone is when, for example, the intelligent boys who shoot their classmates turn out to be from so-called intact families. *But they came from a good family!* Meaning, the parents were married.

All this said, it's still true that children suffer at the hands of their parents whenever there is a divorce. Don't kid yourself. There's a little Medea in all of us.

Euripides' *Medea*, first produced at a dramatic festival in Athens in 431 B.C. (where it received not first, but third, place) is one of the best-loved Greek tragedies, in part because even by modern standards it's savage and extreme, a cautionary tale about what happens when a man underestimates the fury of his ex-wife.

Medea was the daughter of the king of Colchis, a hamlet on the Black Sea, south of the Caucasus Mountains. Charismatic, passionate, and reckless, Medea was a sorceress who could heal as well as harm (the word 'medicine' is derived from her name). When Jason and the Argonauts landed at Colchis to capture the Golden Fleece, Medea fell for Jason in a big way. She was extreme in displaying her feelings. The coveted fleece was owned by Medea's father, whom she eagerly betrayed, as well as the rest of her people, in order to help Jason capture the prize.

(Bad Move #1: Betraying family for a guy. It may seem romantic at the time, but will always be a sticking point when the relationship hits a few bumps.)

Jason and Medea became a hot item. They married and returned to Jason's city, Iolcos, where he was set to assume the throne. Although Jason was the proper heir, Jason's uncle, Pelias, the current ruler, wasn't about to step down now that Jason was back in town. Medea, enraged that her man was being denied what was rightfully his, murdered Pelias.

(Bad Move #2: Helping too much. Medea contributed to her own eventual feelings of resentment and rage by not allowing Jason to run his own life and take his own hard knocks. In addition to her other problems, Medea had some boundary issues.)

After Medea murdered Jason's uncle, they were forced again to flee. We can only imagine how life with Medea was starting to seem from Jason's perspective. The charm of his wife's willingness to murder on his behalf must have been wearing a little thin. Living *la vida loca* is only fun for so long, then it gets exhausting.

When Jason and Medea arrived at Corinth, Jason promptly dumped Medea for yet another princess, this one the daughter of the king.

Euripides' story begins with Medea plotting her revenge. Jason and Medea have a spat that, despite the fact it's 2,400 years old, is eerily prescient of the kind of bickering enjoyed by exes today:

> Jason: This is not the first occasion that I have noticed How hopeless it is to deal with a stubborn temper.

Medea: O coward in every way – that is what I
         call you, With bitterest reproach for your
         lack of manliness.

Medea rants, listing all the things she did for Jason – betrayal, abandoning her city, murder, childbirth. He says he doesn't know what she's getting so upset about. His marrying the princess will give their children a better life. It's not really even *about* another woman, it's about influence and being well-positioned in Corinthian society. It'll be better for all of them. Anyway, he got Medea out of that dump Colchis, so he doesn't know what she's bitching and moaning about.

A part of the story that is frequently deleted in the telling, and that second wives will appreciate, is the first part of Medea's two-part plan for revenge. Medea pretends to reconcile with Jason, and to show her goodwill, sends their sons with a gift of a 'valuable garment' for Jason's new wife, the princess. The princess, unfamiliar with Medea's taste for extreme measures, puts on the robe, and the poison with which Medea has lined the garment takes affect immediately. The princess falls to the floor, body on fire, the robe stuck to her flesh. She dies in agony, in the arms of her father, the king, who is also struck by the poison, and dies as well. Not part of the plan.

Medea realizes she's now trapped into carrying out the second, most heinous part of her plan.

(Bad Move #3: Never construct a revenge plan that has two parts.)

Now, if Medea doesn't take the lives of her own sons, the Corinthians will kill both her and her sons in order to avenge the death of their king. In the play, Medea rushes into her house, offstage. There are two screams, then silence. Jason comes to seek her, believing her only crime is the murder of his wife, the princess.

Jason: You women, standing close in front of this dwelling, Is she, Medea, she who did this dreadful thing Still in the house, or has she run away in flight?

Chorus: O Jason, if you but knew how deeply you are Involved in sorrow, you would not have spoken so.

Jason: What is it? Is she planning on killing me also?

Chorus: Your children are dead, and by their own mother's hand.

Jason: What! That is it? O woman, you have destroyed me!

Chorus: You must make up your mind your children are no more.

Critics of the play, including Aristotle, hated the ending. A magic chariot, provided by the sun god and drawn by dragons, spirits Medea away to Athens. Some claim it's the ultimate example of the *deus ex machina*, others feel it's a commentary on the way the gods intervene in human lives, with apparently no regard for what mortals feel is fair or just.

In any case, Medea gets away with it.

The harm most of us do our children and stepchildren in the name of getting a shred of revenge for a perceived wrong is nothing compared with the antics of Medea, but there are echoes of her intent in our daily acts just the same. I'm not talking about people with true Medea complexes, about parents who physically abuse their children, or launch a full press attack to brainwash their child into hating their ex-spouse (a serious problem called Parental Alienation Syndrome, guaranteed to hurt not the hated ex, but the child, who grows up believing that one half of him – the 'half' he got from his other parent – is hateful, and who will need therapy for a lifetime). I'm talking about the so-called good parents, the normal parents, the parents just trying to get along, as well as the perfect parents (I know you're out there) who can't imagine what I'm on about. They *love* their children, they *worship* their children, they would *never ever ever* use their children to get back at their ex, or their stepchildren to get back at their spouse's ex. This last group is the one that should really watch out; they have no clue how much damage can be done during a Medea moment.

Unlike Medea, who was, after all, a character in a drama, we live and parent in real time. It's less about making tragic and grandiose plans for maximum damage to the ex-spouse, and more about doing the right but subtly annoying thing in real time, tick tock, minute by minute. Being the good parent of a child you share with someone you've come to detest is like trying to quit smoking, or lose weight. You may decide to do it, but it's the simple behavior performed every day that determines success. Do you bum a few puffs off your friend's cigarette or not? Sneak that chocolate chip cookie or not? Allow a snide remark about your ex's inability to pay her rent slip into an otherwise benign conversation you're having with your child, or not? The relentless task demands its own twelve-step program, complete with a set of aphorisms that can be made into bumper stickers.

> When in Doubt, Don't Say Anything.
> It Will Be Bedtime Sooner Than You Think.
> Smile and Shut Up.

But even the best-intentioned divorced parent, who's living under the sort of stress few married people can comprehend, sometimes succumbs to the temptation to zing the ex using her own children. Sometimes, it's only a matter of changing the intonation of your voice, or rolling your eyes. These are the sorts of things that can happen in a Medea moment:

You're chatting on the phone with a friend, and you tell a story about your psycho ex, knowing full well your child is within earshot.

You send your son off for a weekend to his other parent's house, and don't send along a change of clothes, because the other parent has, in the past, neglected to send the clothes home with the child. If you cheerfully explain this to the child, pointing out that the other parent keeps the clothing as a way to avoid buying some with his own money, extend your Medea moment to two.

You are restrained enough not to criticize your child's other parent in front of the child, but happily go to town on the monster truck shows the child's other parent *lives* for.

The other parent phones, and you, who are furious with him for some reason, 'forget' to tell the child he called.

You ask your child to give his dad a message: Where's the child support?

The possibilities for Medea moments are unlimited. I used to doubt the premise put forth by optimistic New Age writing teachers that everyone has it in them to be creative. I believed that everyone had it in them to be derivative. Then I saw the many ways divorced parents use their children to wound their ex-spouse. I now stand corrected.

Once, at the airport, Matthew and I were putting Erica on a plane to visit Matthew's parents in Nevada. It may have been the first time Erica had flown on her own, just after she'd turned seven.

I need to stop and say a word here about Erica: she's impossible to resist. I'm not a carriage-peeper, or a natural lover of children. Not all babies turn me into mush, and just because someone happens to be four years old I don't think everything that comes out of his mouth is some kind of unparalleled Zen wisdom.

Erica is different. She has Matthew's tropical blue eyes and painfully bony knees, where all the complicated inside parts can be seen from the outside. She fancies herself a conversationalist, Miss Personality. Unlike almost every little girl I know, it's not all about Erica. She feels a personal commitment to drawing the other person out in conversation, a trait that normally doesn't manifest itself in girls until they want to get engaged. 'What's your favorite large animal?' is a favorite icebreaker.

One day while Matthew was at a conference for English teachers, Erica asked if we could go to the mall. I told her I didn't like the mall, but she promised it would be fun.

She modeled fringe vests for me at the western store, and let me select which puppy to take out and hold at the pet shop (a lemon-and-white basset hound). She had information to impart about water dragons, who, unlike most lizards, have quite a personality. ('They look at you when you come into the room. Very friendly.') We had personalized place mats made at a cart that specialized in such a thing. She picked out a truck for Philly, a Scottie dog for Katherine, and a unicorn for herself. We bought a sack full of the weirdest candy we could assemble at the Sweet Factory (blue jawbreakers big enough to choke an elephant, tiny Sweet Tarts made for sticking up your nose), and she thought I should get another hole put in one of my ears, so we did that, too.

The only disheartening moment of the day occurred when we were driving home. Alanis Morissette came on the radio. She knew all the words of *You Oughta Know* by heart. She had a high, cartoon-characterish voice. She sang loud and unself-consciously, the way all kids do, even when she got to the part censored on the radio, '. . . are you thinking of me when you fuck her?' I winced. She said, 'That's my mom's favorite song! What's yours?'

'What's my favorite song? My favorite song is "How Can I Miss You When You Won't Go Away?"'

See, a Medea moment.

Erica furrowed her brow, then said, 'What's your favorite white food?'

I digress. In any case, there's a large and growing

population of children with their own frequent-flyer numbers, which provides exes with plenty of opportunity to stretch themselves, expanding on their regular repertoire of Medea moments.

Children travel back and forth between the cities of each parent during the Holy Trinity of split-visitation holidays: Thanksgiving, Christmas break, and Spring break. They fly mostly on the early evening flight the Friday before the vacation begins (or, in the case of Thanksgiving, that Wednesday). They carry on knapsacks packed with treats and toys to play with on the plane, a bright cloth sticker from the airline giving the three-letter code of their destination stuck smack in the middle of their chest.

To send and receive an unaccompanied minor, the sending parent must list the name of the receiving parent when he or she checks in the child at the gate. At the other end, as soon as the plane has landed, the receiving parent must appear with his or her driver's license, or else the child won't be released. There's a lot of opportunity for fun with this system.

Once, Claudia and her mother, Lillian, took Erica down to Disneyland, then sent her back to us a week before they returned, so she wouldn't miss any school. Claudia had refused to give my name to the airline as the picker-upper – a gesture meant to convey that she refused to acknowledge me – even though Matthew had told her that he would be at school and that I would be the one picking up Erica. Instead, she listed only Matthew's name, which forced Erica and me to wait at the gate for three hours with a flight attendant who got paid overtime to baby-sit us.

The day we put Erica on the plane to visit her grand-parents, there were the usual clusters of nervous blended families seeing children off. Mothers dabbing back tears and giving last-minute instructions, fathers grim and sad-eyed looking around above everyone's heads. A flight arrived as we were at the podium arranging Erica's paperwork. The attendant got on the P.A. and began calling for the receiving parents of the arriving children: 'Marvin Taylor, please come to the podium. Debbie McCardle, please come to the podium. Dick Les Wonder, please come to the podiu—'

Matthew and I caught one another's glance. Did you hear what I heard? One thing I could always count on with Matthew: he didn't miss much. The flight attendant, a young Asian woman, stared down at the sheet, then brought it up to her nose, then called over another flight attendant, and together they peered at the piece of paper. The second one started giggling. I knew what I'd heard.

'Excuse me, but I have to be nosy, was that . . .'

'D-I-C-K, then L-E-S, then Wonder, last name,' said the attendant.

You can only imagine, right? Some irate ex-wife

who doesn't want her kid spending time with his dad, her ex. Some woman who did not fare well in the divorce, or she did, but was left for someone younger, for which no amount of retribution is enough. Some woman who had an endless amount of energy for getting her marbles back.

But what about the kid? We didn't see who was the son or daughter of Dick Les Wonder, but let's hope she was only five or six, not eleven, not old enough to know that her dad was the laughingstock of Gate C19. And what complication ensued when Dick Les Wonder showed up and his license said he was Tom Smith? Were he and his child forced to wait until the whole matter was cleared up? If the ex-wife of Dick Les Wonder was not reachable, would the child then be put on the next returning flight?

In mythology and fairy tales, stepmothers have gotten a worse rap than even murderous mothers. There are no exes in 'Snow White' or 'Cinderella', just stepmothers who are cruel and spiteful for no apparent reason. Snow White's stepmother puts Snow White into a deep sleep, and for this infraction she's forced to dance until she dies. Cinderella's stepmother makes her do all the housework, and won't let her go to the ball. In the original Grimm tale, the stepmother's eyes are pecked out at Cinderella's wedding.

In her book *Blending Families*, Elaine Fantle Shimberg writes, '. . . you have been pinned with the stigma of being the "wicked" one even before you have entered into the stepparent fraternity or sorority . . . you are not considered innocent until proven guilty. The burden of proof is on you.'

The noncustodial stepmother is a woman with two lives. Every other weekend, and on an assortment of holidays, children not her own, who may resent her a great deal, tumble into her house, demanding not simply a shift from the regular schedule, but a mental shift. The kids call their stepmother 'her', since they don't know what to call her. They may be sweet, until she asks them to take their feet off the table, and then she is informed that she is not their mother.

'It's nearly impossible to avoid what they tell me is called the Santa Syndrome,' said a woman named Jeannie, a stepmother of three girls, ages seven, nine, and ten. This is Jeannie's first marriage, and she's pregnant with her first child.

'The girls get dropped off by their mom on Friday night, and they're all jazzed up, and their dad, my husband Bill, hasn't seem them all week and there's a feeling of celebration in the air. It's "Let's go out to dinner!" It's "Let's get ice cream!" We feel like a big, raucous gang. The girls are nice to me, as it happens. I don't do any of the real discipline, but when they're in my house I don't feel funny telling them to clear their own places at the table. We get along. It's all a lot of fun, but something weird happens the next day. Everyone sort of sits around and stares at each other. The girls lie around in their pajamas all morning watching cartoons, while Bill and I do our chores. We both work all week, so we don't get much done around the house. But Bill feels guilty. How often does he get to see his daughters? I suggest he just go and maybe sit with them, just talk, I'll make some banana bread or something, and sometimes he gives it a try, but they don't have a lot to talk about, which makes him nervous. So it's off to the movies, or the mall. "Let's go roller-skating!" "Let's go miniature golfing!" And yes, he does buy them Beanie Babies and things they don't need. He can't help it. He just loves them. He's really not trying to buy their affection or any of those other things people accuse weekend dads of trying to do. Then when the weekend's over, and their mom picks them up, she's miffed − I won't say pissed off, or anything, because she is basically a good mother, and doesn't usually go off in front of the girls − because they haven't done their homework, or we kept them up too late, something. I agree with her, as it happens, but what are we supposed to do? And I feel like we have a pretty dream situation. From what I hear, a lot of people have it a lot worse. But even when it's easy, it's hard.'

Jeannie does have a pretty dream situation. Her step-daughters seem to have accepted her, and their biological mother doesn't seem dedicated to making life miserable for Jeannie's husband. And you'll notice Jeannie doesn't spend any time during the weekend trying to put her stepdaughters into a deep sleep or forcing them to scrub bathroom tiles with a toothbrush. But, as Jeannie pointed out, even when it's easy, it's hard.

The fastest-growing family unit in America are divorced fathers with physical custody of their children. While mothers are said to be awarded physical custody about three quarters of the time, and the family court system always has been considered biased against fathers, this is changing. More states are striving for a 'best-interests-of-the-child' stance, and more fathers are actively fighting for custody. When fathers fight, rather than simply acquiesce, they are awarded custody 60 per cent of the time. Since the statistics also point to ex-husbands eventually remarrying, this means there will be more families where the stepmother is married to the custodial parent.

Her stepchildren (or 'skids' – the great abbreviation used on the message boards at theSecondWivesClub.com) don't tumble in every other weekend and expect to be waited on. She is the mother-on-duty, overseeing homework, cooking meals, supervising chores, hosting slumber parties, administering Children's Tylenol, and listening to endless rounds of jokes about butts and farts . . . all for children who are not her own. And, if the recently released studies of Princeton economist Ann Case are to be believed, she is still to be scorned, for despite all of this, she is still up to no good. According to Ms Case, children raised in a household with a stepmother – notice the sinister phrasing: Her mere presence is pernicious – receive less money for food, health, and education than children raised by their biological mothers. Ms Case obviously did not canvas my neighborhood. I'm the wicked stepmom who pays for the braces on my stepdaughter's teeth, her private school tuition, and the special oatmeal soap for her sensitive skin.

I don't think the women I've met during the writing of this book are especially noble. Most are middle-class, college-educated, over their heads financially, stressed out, and overworked. Some are angry. Those I talked with who were full-time stepmothers (for lack of a better term) also usually had biological children, and said they tried to parent their stepkids the way they would want their own children to be parented, should they find themselves in a similar situation. It's the Blended Family Golden Rule. Since over half of today's kids will live in a stepfamily before the age of eighteen, it's a good one to know.

A technical writer named Renata is one of these brave new stepmoms. She works her own hours (sometimes upwards of sixty a week if she's under deadline), and mothers not just Christian, six, from her first marriage, but her two stepchildren, Brendon, nine and Brittney, ten, from her husband Terry's first marriage. Terry was awarded physical custody of his kids shortly after he and Renata were married three years ago. Terry is a contractor, and during the winter, when most of the major remodeling jobs dry up, Renata not only mothers Brendon and Brittney, she also supports them.

When I told her my hypothesis, that more single dads with custody meant, eventually, more stepmoms parenting stepchildren full-time, she was quick to add, 'And don't forget this. An important piece of the puzzle. The dads that do have custody have custody because their ex-wives are losers. I know that sounds harsh. It may be easier for a dad to get custody than it was twenty years ago, but the mother still has to work damn hard to prove that she's incompetent. So what you've got are stepmothers doing the thankless, ball-busting job of raising these kids, while the real mother pays no child support – forget court orders; it takes forever to enforce them and frankly, I think there's a reluctance to go after deadbeat moms – and inevitably turns up to make trouble as it suits her.

'Lori called one night about a year before we finally got custody. It was midnight, her usual time to call. The kids were still living with her in some armpit suburb in Southern California. Her boyfriend Eddie, who was, get this, the best of both worlds, a born-again former junkie, had left her. She'd just lost her job, or her car had been repossessed, and her mother was threatening to kick her out of the house. Nothing out of the ordinary, but Terry saw an opening and said that in light of her situation, why didn't she let Brendon and Brittney come live with us for a year, just until she could get back on her feet.

'Lori was enthusiastic. Too enthusiastic. She wanted to put Brendon and Brittney on a plane the next morning. It was a few days after Thanksgiving and Terry asked her to please wait until the kids' school broke for winter vacation, since they were coming to our house for Christmas anyway. It would give us a chance to get their bedrooms ready, enroll them in school, get Christian used to the idea of having a brother and sister in the house. These are people we're talking about here, not something you'd order from Amazon.com. You don't just stick them on a plane.

'Not good enough. Lori said if Terry wanted the kids, he had to take them now. It turns out Lori was flat broke. Even with Terry's child support she couldn't make the payment on their after-school day care. She couldn't pay for food or gas. She couldn't pay for panty hose.'

I sat up straight when I heard this detail. Calling and begging for ten bucks for panty hose was a Claudia specialty. Maybe they were the same ex-wife. Like the joke about the world's sole existing fruitcake that gets passed around from person to person, maybe there was only one ex-wife who'd been married to the same ten million men, and was now making life dismal for eight million second wives.

Renata continued. 'I could see how anxious Terry was for this to happen. How hopeful he was. It was like having a fish on a line. So I said that if Lori would agree to wait, we would pay for the kids' day care. We sent her a thousand dollars. Am I the stupidest woman alive? Should I be allowed to pass my genetic material on to the next generation? What was I thinking? That white trash bitch hadn't paid Terry back a nickel since I'd known him. Not a penny, and he's always sending her money in addition to the support. Anything she needs. And she's always got some stupid excuse, some reason why she can't do what we do every day of our lives, which is get up in the morning and go to work like adults.

'Despite the fact I hate Lori, I think very highly of her children. It's one of God's greatest mysteries. How a pair of decent children could have sprung from the loins of that hopeless lowlife. Don't get me started on the real question – how could Terry have married her? How? What was he thinking? I asked him once; No, I've asked him about seven thousand times, and you know what he finally said one day, just to get me off his back? "She laughed at my jokes." She laughed at my jokes? This is a reason to get involved with a life-sucker who's going to fuck you over for the rest of your life? "Mental patients laugh at everything!" I told him. Anyway, I worked my butt off. I wanted Brendon and Britt to come to a nice home. I didn't want them to feel like they were just dumped here, like we'd bought some cheap-o futon and stuck them down in the basement. Christian and Brendon would have to share a room, so I painted my study a nice blue and bought some bunk beds. I painted a bookcase for both kids, covered it with stickers of things I knew they liked. Amazon tree frogs and airplanes for Brendon. Elegant little shoes and teacups for Britt.

'The week before they were scheduled to arrive, Lori called in tears every night. Every single night, a zillion phone calls, her weeping, making Terry feel guilty for helping her out. She had quit her newest job, and was keeping the kids out of school, and every day they were going to Disneyland or Magic Mountain or some-the-hell-where. That's how she spent the thousand bucks I insisted Terry send her. Am I an idiot or what? Oh, wait, I already said that. Then, near the end of the week, she phoned and asked for *more* money. She needed money for gas to get to work, panty hose, dog food. Bullshit bullshit bullshit. When Terry said we had sent her all we could, she told Brendon and Britt to get on the extension.

' "I want both of you and your father to hear this at the same time, kids. Your father cares so little for us he refuses to give us money for food. You will not be going to live with him after all." '

9

The Holiday Whammy

Here is a typical Sunday at the Kate and Allie House, after Matthew moved in: Outside, it's raining. In the basement, Matthew is on the phone, arguing with Claudia. He hisses his argument as he loads the washing machine. Hisses, because he's mildly embarrassed he still has to have these arguments at all. The washing machine is never still in this new household. Erica – who stays with us for longer and longer periods of time as Claudia tries to get her goat business off the ground; oh, and she has a new boyfriend – is a blossoming clotheshorse. She tries on potential outfits for school in the morning, and if the top doesn't work, simply drops it in the dirty clothes pile. Erica is apparently a chip off the old block: Matthew wears a pair of Levi's, once, and into the laundry it goes. My approach is more European, more water-wise: Unless I've spilled something on my clothes, or there's some serious

B.O. developing, I wear them until they're dirty. In my pre-Matthew life, in the time after my divorce, I had a small basketful to wash every Sunday, plus my sheets.

Matthew is only doing the laundry so he can hide in the basement with his phone call. He's ashamed, I know, that his past requires so much tending. On the other hand, I'm beginning to realize that Claudia's spectacular and ongoing ineptitude makes him feel needed.

On the main floor, Kiki is sitting at the kitchen table with a glass of red wine, having her own argument over the phone with Mort, her ex. While Matthew hisses, Kiki enjoys a full-throttle yell. She sounds exactly like someone in a movie, and that's intentional. I, myself, find it much more attractive than Matthew's hissing.

Kiki likes to cook us all dinner on Sunday nights, which we'll eat around 10:00, since she has to take a break from cooking to yell at Mort. This floor of the house smells like baked cheese. The TV is on in the living room, the three children lined up on the sofa in a row. Periodically, there's a tussle over the remote. Philly likes to throw himself on the floor and roll around until Mabel the Bad Breath Dog nips him. Then he can shriek, 'The dog bit me!' When no one pays attention, he starts the loop through the living room to the dining room, in one kitchen door and out the other, down the small hall that leads away from the entryway and back into the living room. 'Mabel's got my eye! The dog's got my eye!' The eye in question is a rubber, bloodshot, big blue eye, the size of a golfball.

Erica and Katherine sit shoulder to shoulder, staring at the tube as if Philly wasn't there. Occasionally Erica says 'Philly, I'm the one that's got your eye.' Erica has her own rubber eye. Hers is brown. I think we may have bought them for all the kids together, around Halloween, but it's all starting to run together: the cramped space, the shouting, the hissing, the television, the big dinners, usually featuring cheese, the huge loads of laundry.

Katherine sucks her thumb, changes the channel with the remote when Philly's out of the room. Then Philly returns and screams at Katherine, who he knows has changed the channel from something with Jim Carrey in it to *Rugrats*. Katherine calmly takes her thumb from her mouth and says, 'There's no need to shout.'

On the second floor is me, in our bedroom with the door closed, reading on our bed. Even upstairs I can still hear Kiki lecturing Mort, the refrigerator door opening and shutting, '*Mabel's got my eye! Mabel's got my eye!*', the chittering of the TV, the low thrum of the dryer. In a glass terrarium, on an overturned orange crate near the bed, Mr Blackwell, the rat Matthew gave Katherine for her birthday – trying to make points – sits on his haunches and cracks open a sunflower seed.

It strikes me that this is how I always wind up: in my room, wherever that may be, with the door closed, reading a book on my bed. I've had three main reading positions for almost thirty-five years: on my back, pillow folded and tucked under my head; on my stomach with the book on the flattened pillow; on my knees in the prayer position, book open on the side of the bed. You'd think at my age I'd have a reading chair, not to mention a den, library, or study. In movies, few adults older than the typical impoverished graduate student read on their bed. Don't confuse reading on the bed with reading *in* bed, which most movie adults do before they go to sleep. People whose bed has a headboard and matching nightstand. A lamp that casts an optimistic glow.

I don't remember my book, and it hardly matters, for I am not reading, I'm hiding. It seems that in the hot, klieg light glare of my desire to be with Matthew – who seemed perfect for me, an English teacher, a man who loved words, a man who loved me – I didn't see and, in my love stupor, forgot to look for, that familiar potted shrub pushed just outside the circle of the blazing beam of love: my essential nature.

Oh yeah. That.

As a child I was afraid of neither dark nor silence. The summer going into sixth grade, I dug myself what I called 'my getaway cave' in our backyard, back beneath the clothesline. My cave was a four-by-four-foot hole with a piece of plywood slapped over the top, and some of the sod my dad had just put down in the spring rolled over the top. I dug slots into the open side so I could climb in and out. I found a leftover piece of orange shag carpet in the garage for the floor, brought down a stack of books, including my mom's paperbacks with the foil covers, a flashlight, a tube of Ritz crackers, a jar of peanut butter, and a bottle of Diet Rite cola – my idea of living. This was the same person who as a full-grown adult thought she could tolerate living in a three-bedroom house with six people, a dog, a rat, and the spirits of three exes. Mr Blackwell ran in his wheel all night long.

There's a line I love from *Monty Python and the Holy Grail*: 'No one expects the Spanish Inquisition!' The same can be said about the effect of the holidays on an ex. No one ever expects the Holiday Whammy.

There is no human trait less attractive than self-pity, and exes catch it as easily as head lice in an overcrowded kindergarten where the kids like to trade hats. It's an insidious state, the emotional equivalent of the Escher drawing where the hand is drawing itself. It's a state where one doesn't simply pity oneself for being such a nice, rational person who unwittingly got wrapped up in such an insufferable mess, but one also finds oneself pitying oneself for pitying oneself. Why am I the one who pities myself for plunging in heedlessly? Why am I the one with regrets, something I swore I'd never have? Claudia is also an accomplished self-pitier.

Matthew said that while he couldn't get Claudia to stop writing letters, he had told her that he would allow me to read whatever she'd written (a good strategy; it had the effect of reducing them to one or two a week). Depending on the day, I read them or didn't. When I did, I could always depend on pages of wallowing: Why didn't Matthew love her? Why didn't anyone love her? Was she too fat? Why did Matthew have all the luck? She had no luck. Tigger (the goat, I presume) had intestinal parasites. Kanga had chronic mastitis. What was she to do? What would become of her? What could she do to get him back?

Matthew is not a self-pitier, and it's one of his finest qualities. He doesn't think it does any good, nor is it becoming. In any case, he believed that all the mistakes he'd made along the way (I wish I was talking about something a little less banal than marrying Claudia) were somehow necessary to get him to the point where he was ready to have a world-class romance with me. Sweet, huh?

In any case, it was the specter of Christmas that had us even more discombobulated than usual.

Every year, women's magazines publish service features about how to get through the holidays. How to cope with holiday depression, how to cope with holiday demands. Greedy children, the onslaught of caloric possibilities, loneliness, existential anguish.

For exes the season is even more rife with emotional land mines. Your normal holiday blahs and blues are squared or cubed – those pesky exponents again – depending on the number of exes orbiting your relationship. You experience general holiday malaise overlaid with memories of the holiday as it was celebrated with the ex. Or, depending on the nature of your marriage the way the holiday was *ruined* by the ex. And if it was ruined by the ex, sometimes even that seems worthy of nostalgia. A week before Christmas, when I was madly ordering everything I possibly could by mail, having waited until the last minute like I always do, Matthew had the nerve to reminisce about how Claudia loved Christmas, how she was always done with her shopping by Labor Day.

Having given up on my own personality as bulwark against shooting my mouth off in a way I would later regret, I had started watching *Masterpiece Theatre* religiously on Sunday nights, hoping to be able to emulate the long-suffering British heroines that populate the *Masterpiece Theatre* world. It might have worked if I had been clamped inside a corset, or had some fringe on my cuff with which to fiddle. Instead, I slammed shut the FAO Schwarz catalog and said, 'God, how anal can you get?'

Matthew nodded. No argument there. It was one of the things that drove him crazy. Still, he lowered his eyes, smiled to himself. 'Yup.'

How to compete with that smile? When it comes

to holidays, especially Christmas, which is always only magical and heartwarming in retrospect, the past trumps the present. The manic shopping for stuff the kids will have lost interest in by the end of Christmas Day, the scandalous amount of money spent for said stuff, the elaborate, expensive meals everyone picks at, preferring instead to feast on chocolate Santas and Ruffles with French onion dip (though if one simply gave up and let the snacks be the meal it would be sacrilege), the low-level sadness that permeates the entire month of December, are somehow never part of Christmas memories. As soon as one Christmas recedes into the past, it reverts to representing hope; the current Christmas staring you in the face is nothing but hassle.

For my ex and me, Christmas was never as luridly consumeristic as it is for many people. In the same way we prided ourselves on never fighting, we also felt smug because we never overspent. The words, 'You shouldn't have!' never left either of our lips. We bought witty wind-up toys and refrigerator magnets for each other's stockings, which were respectably filled, but never brimming over. When I dig for something heartbreaking about my own Christmases past, what comes up is the memory of my ex dutifully cooking his Christmas Eve prime rib. On our last Christmas together he cooked his best one ever, so tender you could cut it with the side of your fork. Now that brings tears to my eyes.

Matthew's memories of Christmas with Claudia are, as you might imagine, dramatic, chaotic, and financially disastrous. They involve arguments in traffic with Claudia getting out of the car at a red light and starting to walk home in the middle of freezing rain that was threatening to turn any minute to ice.

One ex-wife I know said one of the things she missed most about holidays with her ex was the constant domestic bickering about spending money on presents. 'For one thing,' she said, 'I used to get so upset about our fighting I never had to worry about putting on weight. Now I make fudge, and eat it myself.'

Kiki had her own Holiday Whammy to contend with: Philly was going to spend Christmas in Arizona with Mort and his parents this year, which had her feeling both deserted and pissed off, even though it was part of the so-called Parenting Plan. On Christmas Day, Kiki would get to sit around watching Matthew and me open the kind of intimate presents new lovers traditionally buy for one another while ducking Claudia's phone calls, which would come about every twenty minutes, since naturally she had purchased Erica many toys that required batteries, and who better to help her figure out where, exactly, the batteries went, than Matthew, the only person in the entire state who might have this information?

Katherine would be spending Christmas Eve with us, and Christmas Day with her dad. He would come pick her up around ten, after we'd opened our presents, and we would stand around on the front porch feeling uncomfortable and forlorn. I would try to make amends by giving my ex an unwrapped six-pack of a microbrew beer (not his favorite, because I was careful not to send any hidden messages), and he would stand there awkwardly cradling it in his arms.

And it's not simply Christmas that delivers the Whammy. There's always Easter. Fourth of July. Mother's Day and Father's Day, natch. Birthdays. The wedding anniversary – it goes without saying – is a rough day for millions of exes.

Even unimportant federal holidays with their mall sales and silly parades can prime the nostalgia pump. Not to mention private anniversaries. The day the ex proposed! The day we got caught in a landslide in Costa Rica! It all serves not only to remind you of your own failed marriage, but, if you're a ruminating sort, the folly of the entire institution.

There are two ways of combating the Holiday Whammy. The first is to never get divorced in the first place; the second is to get married and divorced so often that there are too many holidays and attendant memories to keep track of. Eventually they all run together, and you can't remember which poignant moment went with which spouse.

10

On Divarriage

One of the purposes of books like this is to reassure the reader, to make things seem if not solvable, then simpler than you might otherwise imagine. Manageable, if nothing else. Here is something that will make your life easier, especially if you're not an ex (and therefore out of shape when it comes to the never-ending emotional bench press that is life in exville) and you are thinking of moving in with or marrying someone who is divorced. It may seem obvious, *Don't assume if someone tells you he's divorced it means he's unattached*. Divorce and disengagement often have as much in common as apples and elephants.

The divarried are a subspecies of exes whose postmarital relationships are the equivalent of the washer-dryer, an invention that doesn't sound as if it would ever work, but nevertheless enjoyed a limited popularity in the 1960s, the same time a lot of other unworkable things, like wife-swapping, were making the rounds in suburbia. It was a single tub that filled first with water, then, with hot air. Simple. Except the clothes never got quite clean or quite dry. In the same way, the divarried live in a limbo where they're not married, but also not divorced. Or, if you're the glass-half-full type, a limbo where they're both divorced and married.

Laundry seems to provide an abundance of metaphors for this dilemma. Consider this: For the past year or so there has been a wicker laundry basket with broken handles sitting in my basement next to the washing machine. This is the lost-sock basket, and every clean sock whose mate is MIA gets dropped into the basket. The basket is the lost-and-neglected-sock repository. Once in a while I sort through the sock basket, but only in order to see if there are any pairs that can be matched up and put away. I almost never throw away the single socks that have been in there for months.

The divarried treat their exes as if they are spare socks. The divarried are those who are separated, who are technically exes, but who haven't gotten around to doing the paperwork yet. Or people who have done the paperwork, but still rely on each other as if they were married. You've left your ex or your ex has left you. Some time has passed, and you haven't gotten back together, but you have yet to rule out getting back together. You're still attached. You still have one sock. You don't dare throw it away, because what if the other one turns up? What if the other one has temporarily been lost between the washer and the dryer? What if it's sitting at the bottom of the drawer? What if you leave the partner who couldn't be relied upon, then suddenly he turns over a new leaf, or meets a new woman, and he becomes what you've always wanted, someone reliable? Luckily, you haven't tossed away the whole relationship yet. Or you have, only to discover you shouldn't have. The truth is most of the time you have to bite the bullet, toss out the single sock, and if you stumble upon its mate, toss that one out too. Or turn it into a dust rag.

Mindi, who by her own admission barely made it through high school, worked her entire adult life as a waitress at a three-star restaurant. Her uniform was chic: black pants and a white dress shirt. It was a great job for someone in her twenties, who didn't mind the weird hours and impending bunions, but Mindi was thirty-four, with two children in a private school where there were no other mothers who smelled like pommes frites. Her divorce from Walt, a public defender and aspiring triathlete who met Someone Else (Mona, an open-water swimmer) was less nasty than most, in part because their split was not a true divorce. They were exchanging their marriage for a divarriage, the same way they once traded in the sedan for the SUV. Walt, believing he was being modern, reasonable, and a cut above those other jerks who complain about getting taken to the cleaners by their ex-wives, agreed to Mindi's suggestion that in exchange for her not seeking maintenance, he would put her through college. The theory was similar to that of the Peace Corps: Don't give people bread; teach them to bake it!

The outcome was not nearly so uplifting. Mindi, who never wanted the divorce, now had two reasons to pester Walt at all hours of the day and night: their children, and her course work. Would he proofread her term paper on 'Tintern Abbey'? Could he spare an hour to quiz her on the parts of a plant for her biology midterm? Was he available to meet for a drink to celebrate her 3.5 GPA? After all, he *was* paying for it. She had stopped being his wife, and started being his investment, a much murkier proposition. At the beginning of Mindi's junior year, Mona, fed up with feeling as if she and Walt were sending a daughter of their own through college, left him for a man who truly was divorced.

Divarriage sounds as if it might be a situation invented by baby boomers, the entire lot of us wanting to have our cake and eat it too. Like adultery, however, we hardly invented it. I once had an eighty-seven-year-old landlady named Jolene, who was famous in our fourplex for wandering around naked in the early-morning hours, throwing bits of old food into the snarl of blackberries that grew on the hill in back of the building. She called this composting. She had an eighty-eight-year-old ex-husband, Donald, who'd diddled a young woman in the steno pool sometime back in the 1940s. (What is the steno pool, anyway? Does anyone born after 1965 have the remotest idea?) Jolene divorced Donald. Jolene never forgave Donald. Jolene never left Donald, either. They didn't live together, but twice a week for more than forty years, Donald would come to the building, even after he'd had both hips replaced, and do minor repairs that involved climbing on ladders, shimmying into the crawl space, spraying for bees – all penance for his crime. Then she'd make him dinner, and they would sit out on the redwood deck that overlooked the hill of blackberries and argue for old time's sake about the stenographer, whose name neither one of them could remember.

There are divarried couples in which one still pays the other's rent, who still send each other birthday presents, whose shoulders are perpetually available for the ex to cry on. Divarrieds put one another down on forms that require emergency contact numbers. They list one another, still, as beneficiaries.

A dermatologist I know – rich, clever, a kick-boxer and quilter – let her ex move back in with her temporarily while his relationship with the woman he left her for broke up. Another ex, a writer, has dictated in his will that his ex-wife will serve as the executrix of his papers. I asked, 'What do you think she'll do when she finds your hundreds of journal pages about how unbearable she was to live with, about the woman you met when you took your kids to the pool in the summer, about the lap dancers?' He paused for a moment. 'I can't say I ever thought about that. I just know that she's the one to do the job.'

Last night I was reading *Elle* in the bathtub and came across a mention of a show of Picasso's ceramics at the Metropolitan Museum of Art. 'As boyfriends go, you could do better, but the guy sure knew his way around a hunk of Play Doh' was the lead, and I studied it for some time. Why, exactly, did the writer think Picasso was such a bad choice on the love front? Sure, we all know that Picasso was a Promethean monster of ego and appetite. He was narcissistic, moody, self-pitying, and more than occasionally cruel, but hey, you want to be with an artistic genius and one of western civilization's first genuine celebrities, you'll have to put up with some nonsense. There are many women who put up with the same unsavory traits in guys who can't paint the bathroom, much less *Guernica*.

What rankles about Picasso's love life, I think, is not that he was cruel or selfish, but that the foundation of his sadism, his habitual amatory M.O., was refusing to disentangle himself fully and completely from the women he dumped. Picasso's life was a living testament to the power of the institution of divarriage. He had six major women in his adult life and technically never left any of them. He always waited for the woman on the way out to get the hint herself and try to leave (note use of the word 'try').

The hint always appeared in his paintings. If you were dating Pablo, and suddenly you stopped looking like a voluptuous bathing beauty and started showing up on the canvas as a misshapen hag with two noses, daggerlike tears spurting out of your hideous eyes, it was time to pack your bags. For he would, by this time, already be running around with someone else.

If you didn't leave (none of his women did), you'd weep, probably go somewhat mad, and he would move out, offended at your shrewish, possessive displays. Then he would write you, the woman who should have been his ex, letters reassuring you that he still loved you – gushy, over-the-top notes that could only have been written by a Spaniard – thereby keeping you still and forever in his orbit, still divarried to him. But, of course, you were not married, or even living together, and when you began to get on his nerves, he would remind you of this. As a result, Picasso's romantic history reads like *The House That Jack Built*.

First there was Picasso's first wife, whom he married relatively late, at thirty-four, and never divorced. Olga

Koklova was a perfectly presentable if mediocre ballerina with the Ballet Russe. That marriage tanked within a year; one of the greatest personalities in modern history falling into the same old trap we all do: reasoning that even though you might be walking into a marriage with the wrong person, he or she might turn out to be the *right* wrong person, a person who may not be able to make you happy, but will at least be able to offer you a rest from your own demons. This rarely works, however, and it didn't work for Picasso.

Before Picasso moved out of the apartment he shared with Olga, he took up with a girl he spied crossing the street, Marie-Thérèse Walter, age seventeen, a protojock who should have been born in a time when she could have played professional hockey. Picasso loved her frisky, girlish quality, which vanished upon the birth of their daughter, Maya. By the end of that year, baby Maya still in her arms, Marie-Thérèse was replaced by dark-eyed surrealist photographer and mouthy intellectual, Dora Maar. Maar then became the primary mistress, while Marie-Thérèse – in a sports metaphor she surely would have appreciated were she not being driven insane by Picasso – was demoted to the second string. This became Picasso's lifelong habit, always taking secondary and even tertiary lovers, not unlike a football coach who occasionally likes to mix things up by throwing in the benchwarmers.

Predictably, Dora began to have a problem with her

lover's divarriages. Demanding and opinionated herself, she began to take issue with the fact that when she and Picasso would vacation together in the South of France, he would inform *both* second-string mistress Marie-Thérèse and estranged wife Olga where she and Picasso were headed (in some cases actually installing the wife or the other mistress in a vacation flat near their own). The situation was like that of a Hollywood western: This town ain't big enough for the both of us, or in this case, for *all* of us. The women would frequently run into one another on the street. Dora threw several notable fits, and was transformed into Picasso's official weeping woman.

One night in 1943, Picasso and Dora were eating supper at La Catalan in Paris. Picasso was sixty-two; I don't know how old Dora was, but you can be sure she was several decades older than the girl her man noticed sitting across the restaurant, the girl at whom Picasso pointed, saying, 'There is my next lover!' or something equally subtle and reassuring. Dora sniffed, or guzzled her absinthe, or wept into her hands, or something, because almost immediately, like a guest on a late-night television talk show, she was moved down a chair to make way for Françoise Gilot, age twenty-one.

The situation with Picasso, Olga, Marie-Thérèse, Dora, Françoise, and the hottie-of-the-week with whom he was messing around, would have made an excellent French farce. One of those plays that features a lot of door slamming. For after the nubile charms of Françoise wore off, Picasso took up with a seventeen-year-old, Genevieve La Porte, who came to interview him for her school newspaper. That Picasso was still married to Olga, had a child with Marie-Thérèse, still promised Dora that she was the only one, was openly in love with Françoise (who was young enough to be his granddaughter) provided no incentive for Picasso to pass up an affair with yet another, still younger, girl.

Dora eventually found herself institutionalized, her rages checked by electroshock therapy. Picasso, openly disgusted by her apparent weakness, but uninterested in letting her go and putting her out of her misery, bought a house for her, even though their love affair was long over. He'd traded a small still-life for it. His gift was a way both to solidify forever their bond, and to put her out to pasture.

The Picasso saga continues on a few decades longer – there is the death of Olga, his wife, then an unlikely late-in-life remarriage to Jacqueline Boc, a clingy, unremarkable store clerk, barely more than a teenager when they met. Picasso, of course, is about 750 years old by this time – but you get the picture.

I tested my divarriage theory on an ex I was supposed to be interviewing. I'd been particularly interested in speaking to Janice, because our situations were so similar.

Janice, a chiropractor in a large midwestern city, enjoyed a relatively calm relationship with her own ex-husband. They'd often commented to each other that they were better exes than they were friends. But Janice's ex-wife-in-law, that is, the ex-wife of her new husband, Lon, also a chiropractor, still bought Lon boxers. Whenever Lon's ex-wife ran across a pair that reminded her of Lon – it should be noted that just the fact they were boxers reminded her of Lon – she bought them for him.

'I don't think it's a coincidence that she just *happens* to come across a pair he *has* to have every time she feels like she wants a closer connection. She gives them to him in a shopping bag the next time they do the kid exchange. I told Lon I thought her giving him presents all the time, and boxer shorts at that, was inappropriate. He said they weren't a present because they weren't *wrapped*.'

'Of course,' I said, 'That's because they're divarried.'

When she looked as if she'd misheard me, I said, 'As in divarriage.'

'Of course the French would have a word for something like that,' she said.

The French? I made it up!

11

Mrs Gaspin, C'est Moi

Two weeks after Christmas, Claudia began to get mail at our house. A bank statement arrived on a day the weather man predicted ice. Her first name, Matthew's last name, our address. Claudia said she would always keep Matthew's last name, so that everyone knew who Erica's mother was. (She would drop it the moment she landed a man disenchanted with her messy past, but that would be later).

It was a Saturday. I brought the statement up to Matthew, who was playing a game on the computer, also in our bedroom, remember, along with the bed, the dresser, the bookcase, a television, two nightstands, Mr Blackwell's terrarium.

I said, 'I'm writing, "return to sender." Call her and tell her we refuse to accept this.'

He said, 'She told me she thought it'd be a good

idea to have a contact address in Portland. For the business.'

I said, 'For the business? For what business, Matthew? For this bogus goat cheese business, or whatever the hell excuse she's using to indulge her pathological need to have as many mammals around her as possible. Did I tell you the American Psychiatric Association has actually come up with a legitimate diagnosis for people like her?'

He said: 'You told me.'

I said: 'What'd she buy last month with your child support check? Instead of buying new shoes for Erica? A turkey, was it?'

He said: 'I don't remember.'

I said: 'An emu. Remember? She had to call here at 11:30 at night to ask you what she should name it. She's insane, Matthew. And I don't want her using *my* address. I'm going to call her right now and tell her this has got to end.'

Matthew said nothing.

Of course, I was the one who was now insane. I was starting to sound like Claudia. I heard it in my own voice. Maybe before Matthew had met Claudia she was normal, and he'd driven her insane, like Charles Boyer did to Ingrid Bergman in *Gaslight*.

Up until this point my phone contact with Claudia had been minimal, per Matthew's request. I never answered the Red Phone, and had become too skittish to answer the house phone. The times I had answered, she'd been unnervingly upbeat. Even if she had only moments before left one of her signature drop-dead phone messages, she would pretend as if she hadn't.

'Hiiiiii-eeeeeee!' She never identified herself. I was simply supposed to know. And after the first few times, I did know, mostly because everyone else who called said something like, 'Hi, it's Ed. Is Kiki there?' When Katherine's father called, he never failed to identify himself, polite as ever.

Matthew was afraid that whatever I would say would enrage Claudia, that Claudia would feel that my involvement in this was none of my business, and in retaliation she would disappear with Erica.

'Disappear? *Disappear?* Claudia's not going anywhere,' I'd say. 'Disappear without a trace, which, incidentally, means without a phone? We should be so lucky.'

But I was reluctant to get on the phone, because of Erica, because Claudia did have a history of driving into cinder block walls, and so I did nothing. I wept. I lost more weight. I developed anemia, which lead to a condition called pica. For reasons science has failed to understand, a lack of iron in the blood creates a craving for nonfood. Children who have it eat dirt or paint. I liked uncooked elbow macaroni. Inside my head it made the loudest crunch I'd ever heard, so loud, it drowned out all my thoughts.

What I really wanted to do was throttle Claudia, pull

her hair, knock out some teeth, kick her in the ribs, if I could find them under all that fat, clonk her on the head so hard that all her past with Matthew, all those memories of − well, arguing − but the good ones too ran out one ear and were left forever pooled on the sidewalk.

I imagine you're thinking what I was beginning to think. Probably, you were way ahead of me. Probably, at my first mention of the Underpants Episode, you thought, 'Uh-oh. Run away now, run away now.' You probably figured out that Matthew was not, in fact, asking Claudia to stop sending, stop writing, stop calling, stop bugging. That he was, in fact, encouraging her in some way. That he and Claudia were not divorced, but divarried.

In his defense, it must be said that it took very little to encourage Claudia. Veiled anything − hostility, loathing, derision, criticism − remained as opaque as an eggshell. There's no subtext in Claudia's world, no overwhelming unsaid that threatens to quash the conversation there and then. Likewise, the vaguest noninquiry, 'How are you?', is apt to trigger impassioned updates on her weight problem, hemorrhoids, depleted bank account, newly minted plans to move back to Portland.

Yes. Into our neighborhood, in fact.

The phone message: 'There's a really cute house not a mile away from you on a quarter acre where I can still have my goat farm. You were right all along, Eeyore. The schools are better in Portland, and Erica really needs a good school, maybe even that private one, so she doesn't get lost in the shuffle. Could you do me a favor and send me the Classifieds so I can start job hunting?'

After this phone call I lost my composure for the rest of the relationship. This business about Erica needing a better school so she wouldn't get lost in the shuffle were my words almost exactly. Obviously, Matthew had passed them off to Claudia as a thought he'd had, the better not to drag my name into the conversation and start an argument. Hedge, hedge, hedge.

Claudia a mile away from us in Portland. Walking distance! Claudia dropping by anytime, all the time. Claudia pitching a fit on our front lawn. Claudia marching into the house to holler at Matthew.

Another message two days later.

'Hiiiieeee. Just wondering where the Classifieds are. Have you sent them yet? I thought I'd asked nicely like you told me to. You do know, Matthew, that if you had asked me to send you something, I would have FedExed them that day.'

May I remind you she lived forty-six miles away? The Classifieds she was so desperate for were in *The Sunday Oregonian*, which she could easily pick up herself in Salem. She signed off saying, 'I can't wait until we're together again.'

'She doesn't mean together with *me*,' Matthew explained, 'she means so Erica and I can see each other more. It's good for Erica to spend time with her dad. Claudia's very sensitive to that kind of thing. She feels that a lot of her problems have to do with not having had a father herself.'

'Don't *defend* her. Don't explain her to me. She's fucking insane and always has been. She's not high-strung. She's not *Tigger*. She's some horrible incurable virus. And she's not a great mother, like you keep saying. You say that so you can justify her raising your only child. She's a terrible mother, in fact. She uses Erica like she always has to get to you. No good mother does this. Hasn't it ever occurred to you that that's why she got pregnant in the first place? So she could hold her over your head? I can't believe she leaves messages like this. I cannot believe it. Can't she see you're living with somebody else? She does know we're living together, doesn't she? Where does she imagine I'll be when you two are "together again"? If you didn't want to leave her, you shouldn't have left her.'

I'm dangerously on the edge of a full-blown rant. I am Adele the Dog Lady. I am Mrs Gaspin, minus the ankle bracelet. A snippet of rant can be titillating, the way a movie preview is, but the endless harangue, which ex-wives and women with ex-wives-in-law are capable of getting caught up in like an inexperienced rafter caught in an eddy, is never anything less than off-putting.

To satisfy my need to rant, while at the same time sparing you the pain of having to read it, I present instead an index to an imaginary book-length tirade against this poor woman whose greatest crime was not getting over her divorce. And cutting up my underpants.

THE INDEX

American Express card
- running up charges on joint account still shared with Matthew as means of revenge
- qualifying for, Matthew will never again

bankruptcy
- always on the verge of, then buys some livestock to console herself

boyfriends
- married fellow goat breeder, brief fling with
- reverting to obsessive pursuit of Matthew after being unceremoniously dumped by
- my fervid, nightly prayers that she get another one, soon

child support payments
- as deposited by Matthew directly into her account on the first of the month

- profanity regarding appearance of funds in afternoon instead of first thing in the morning
- inability of Claudia to spend wisely (see livestock)

Erica

- as eternal pawn in game of Get Matthew Back
- as something Matthew intentionally saddled Claudia with (according to Claudia) in order to ruin her life
- as truly adorable munchkin who deserves better

finances (see also livestock)

- as excuse to make panicked phone call day or night

'fuck'

- you, asshole, as favorite epithet
- most popular phrase left on answering machine
- constant use of as continuous reminder of charming nature of personality

livestock

- purchase of, as indication of depression
- existence of, as an excuse to call Matthew and beg for money to pay large-animal vet
- existence of, as the reason she can never afford panty hose for myriad job interviews

panty hose

- need for as excuse to call several times a week

quitting job in a huff
- chronic habit of, when she's actually expected to work for her paycheck
- effect of, on frequency of phone calls begging for money
- effect of, on frequency of phone calls begging Matthew to advise her on finding a job where she doesn't hate everyone

threats, generic
- to show up on doorstep and have it out once and for all
- to take Erica and disappear!
- to leave Erica with her mother and disappear!
- eventual disbelief of

threats, murder
- made to Matthew
- made to me
- made to boss (see quitting job in a huff)

Winnie-the-Pooh
- the thought of, ruined forever

Like most of my relationships, the one with Matthew was over before it ended. I cannot point to one precipitating event. It was like developing an allergy to peanut butter. It's not the first peanut butter sandwich, or the second, but too many peanut butter sandwiches create an increased hypersensitivity to peanuts, and the next thing you know your face swells up and you can't breathe and you know without a doubt that peanuts, formerly harmless, are now capable of killing you.

Every morning that winter was uniformly gray and drippy. The gold and plum-red leaves of the sugar maples sat like Wheaties in the gutters, clogging the storm drains and causing minor floods. I wish I could report that I got in the habit of staying in bed until noon, or developed a hankering for daytime television, or started obsessively ordering cubic zirconia tennis bracelets off the Home Shopping Network, or something, anything, that signifies depression in a grand and splashy manner, but I didn't. I trudged along, getting up faithfully at 6:30 every morning to get Katherine, and sometimes Erica, ready for school. I had half a bagel with a small swipe of cream cheese, two cups of coffee with milk, no sugar. I got myself dressed, never forgoing the mascara or mouthwash, even when there were four of us in the bathroom at the same time, all jockeying for space in front of the mirror.

I dropped Katherine at preschool, and arrived at my office by 8:30 A.M. The only evidence that I was stunned with despair was the fact I wasn't writing. I sat in my office morning after morning and stared out the third-floor window at a very tall, very thin cedar that whipped around in the gusty wind.

It was a middle-class nervous breakdown: no theatrics or drugs, no long trip to an alpine spa where someone else monitored my fragile mental health. Matthew and I still went to movies, cooked together, made love and jokes, argued about which was better, *War and Peace* or *Crime and Punishment*.

But as every ex who has an ex-wife-in-law (which Claudia essentially was, even though Matthew and I weren't married) or an ex-husband-in-law, not to mention stepchildren from various marriages underfoot, as well as a convoluted maintenance/child support arrangement, will tell you, however beloved the new partner is in theory, the movies, the meals, the laughs, the passion the two of you share for growing succulents or collecting vintage salt and pepper shakers, even, alas, the mind-blowing sex, eventually begins to shrink in proportion to the ongoing need to tend to obligations created in the past.

Consider for a moment the movie *Independence Day*. Your mutual love of salsa dancing is the Empire State Building; your exes and everything attached to them is the seven mile-wide spaceship hovering over you, blocking out the sun.

My sassy, never-divorced mother, were she alive, would have been able to predict the problems of my involving myself with Matthew. My mother would have known that when you marry a man (or live with one; they didn't really have cohabitation in her day) you not only take on his family, you take on his ex-wife as well. This seems so obvious, I feel ridiculous even pointing it out. I hadn't thought things all the way through, however. I'd imagined that after several months of Matthew and I living together, Claudia would figure out that Matthew was gone, would realize the futility of phoning so much, and fall off the face of the earth.

There was a larger, overarching problem, something I wished I'd considered seriously months before. One day as I was at my office staring out the window through the slanting rain, I realized that Claudia's compulsion for connection wasn't simply habit, strategy, or a deliberate campaign of terror. It really wasn't. It was more serious than this. Claudia was not desperate to hang on to Matthew because he was Matthew, a former backstroking star and English teacher, with a habit of rescuing losers, and a love of hot fudge sundaes.

This explained how she could regularly profess undying love for him – it was almost a nervous tic – but remain unconcerned when, for example, he'd been sleeping wrapped around the toilet all night, sick with food poisoning. Dry heaves were never an excuse for failing to return a phone call. The fact that Matthew went to the movies, slept in, got stuck somewhere with a flat tire – in short, had a life – failed to impress her.

In a sense, he didn't exist, except in his role as *husband*.

It was imperative that Claudia maintain the illusion that she was somehow hanging on to him because however threadlike the connection really was, the mere fact of him returning her phone calls prevented her from experiencing the most horrific of female experiences: for if Claudia lost Matthew for good, she would become her mother.

When her father left, Claudia was the exact age Erica was now. No child support, no dozens of dramatic phone calls, no silly toys or packages of Sweet Tarts sent to the child Claudia simply because he was thinking of her. Claudia has no memory of him.

Once I had a clear realization of this, however, it was too late for empathy. Not that any woman is able to drum up much in the way of real compassion for her predecessor. 'Women do not want to be one bead on a long necklace of wives,' says novelist Carolyn See.

Amanda, a manicurist I know who, interestingly enough, has a degree in archaeology, is an ex-wife involved with an ex-husband. Both have sons roughly the same age. 'I cannot stand being second. I don't know what it is. We don't expect our husbands to be *virgins*, but I simply can't cope with the fact that there was someone there before me who knows how to fold his shirts and how he likes his eggs. I suppose an old girlfriend could have known all this, but for some reason it's not the same as a wife. A wife, even an ex-wife, can sashay in at any moment and throw her weight around. Despite divorce, there's still that "I was here first" thing. Like homesteading or something.'

One night Matthew was at parent-teacher conferences. It was just Kiki and I, and a rented movie, *Manhattan*. I was lying on the sofa and Kiki sat sideways in the rocking chair, her legs slung over one arm. Outside, the rain spit against the windows in fits and starts. The Red Phone rang upstairs, then the house phone rang, then the Red Phone. Kiki and I traded glances.

'*God*.' She rolled her eyes.

'I'm in hell,' I said. I was secretly pleased. I now looked forward to Claudia's episodes. They gave me fresh material, new things to complain about, new scenes to reenact for anyone who would listen. Magazine editors I worked with over the phone, women and men I'd never met, had all heard Claudia's greatest hits. Kiki was privy to each and every exchange. We analyzed Claudia's phone messages as if we were forensic experts, mulling over the meaning of her phrasing, the tone of her voice. There was never a call that wasn't evidence of her insanity. Even her most neutral, business-like calls – and there were a good number of these – were part of her insidious plan to put Matthew off guard, to show him that she was 'better', to break us up, get him back, drive him crazy, something.

This time she'd left two messages upstairs on the Red Phone's answering machine, and one on the house phone's voice mail. What a happy development. I couldn't wait until Matthew got home and I could tell him that she was on the rampage again, making my life impossible. Here Kiki and I were, trying to watch a movie, and Claudia was ruining things yet again.

The first two messages were similar. 'Hi, call me, it's an emergency, something really bad has happened, call me. Bye.' On the first message her voice broke on 'bad'. Her nose was so plugged from crying she sounded like Elmer Fudd. The third message went, 'I know you probably are going to hear this and just blow me off. Do not blow me off, Matthew. This is really serious. Something really bad has happened. Call me. Bye.'

Kiki made some microwave popcorn. We stood in the kitchen eating it from its finger-burning bag.

'It's gotta be something with Erica,' said Kiki. 'Erica's broken her arm or something.'

'Oh, yeah, the Mad Cow and all her medical emergencies. Why is her being psychotic never one of them?' 'Mad Cow' was a nickname a novelist friend of mine had coined after I'd made some joke about wishing Claudia would come down with mad cow disease. 'Remember the time she called and said it was an emergency when she'd gotten a flat and didn't know how she was going to get to work the next day, because, *of course*, she didn't have a spare.'

I spent twenty more minutes reminding Kiki what

she'd already heard a half-dozen times before – that Claudia thought a rash was reason enough to call an ambulance.

At that moment, I had a vision of the future. This could go on for ever. Really for ever, which is a terrifying proposition. My friend Sarah recently told me about the ongoing battles between her mother, Lenore, and her stepmother, Vera. Lenore had left Sarah's father in the 1960s for another man. He then had married Vera, and had been married to her for exactly thirty years when he died. A few months after the funeral, Vera came to stay with Sarah here in Portland.

At 6:30 A.M. the morning after Vera left, Lenore phoned Sarah.

'Well,' said Lenore, 'any news?'

'Yeah, Dad's still dead.'

'How did she look? Is she still a drunk?'

'Mom, could you give her a break? Her husband just died.'

'He was my husband first! And don't you dare forget it. Vera is nothing but cheap goods. And that drinking problem. How could he find her attractive? Booze is hard on a woman's looks, and she didn't have a hell of a lot to start with.'

Lenore and Vera are both in their seventies.

In my vision of the future, Matthew and I are eighty-four and ninety. We've just returned from a cruise through the Panama Canal. I have artificial hips and Matthew has had cataract surgery. Neither of us can hear very well. We come home to our rent-controled apartment to find eighty-seven phone messages. They all say more or less the same thing.

'It'd be nice if I could get a fucking phone call returned once in a fucking while,' Claudia says in a quavery voice. She's seventy-nine.

'Does she always have to call!' I shriek.

'What?' yells Matthew.

'Can't she just get a life!'

'WHAT?'

Kiki and I were still in the kitchen, leaning against the counters, cracking ourselves up. We moved on to discuss Claudia's goat farm, which she'd thought to call Hundred Acre Woods Nubian Goat Farm. We scoffed at her lack of originality, as if we had dozens of original and witty farm names just waiting for farms to attach them to. We could riff on the livestock thing for hours. It had become a joke around the house. Kiki would come in from a hard day at work, fish a bottle of wine out of the cupboard, and say, 'God, I've had a lousy day. I know just the thing to perk me up. A nice hog.'

Suddenly, we heard three quick *clomps* outside, the sound of someone coming up the sagging front porch steps, then a polite knock on the door. It was the civil knock of the neighbor who comes over once a week or so to borrow an egg. It was not the knock of Katherine's father, my ex, who does the shave-and-a-hair-cut-two-bits knock, or Philly, who doesn't need to knock, but does anyway, just for fun. He knocks and yells.

I went to the door. There was a woman on the porch. Her red curls shone under the porch light. Claudia.

In all this time, Claudia and I had never stood face to face. After the Underpants Episode, when she was escorted from Matthew's house by her friends, she'd never met my gaze. Since then, there had been various pick-ups and drop-offs, but one or the other of us was always in another part of the house, or waiting in a parked car.

I saw everything in less than a minute. Claudia was shorter than I remembered, perhaps 5'2", and more peculiarly shaped, with heavy forearms and wrists, large calves and ankles, but small feet. I wondered if she had a thyroid problem, or gout. (Did anyone under ninety get gout? What was gout?) She wore An Outfit – clearly it was An Outfit, not something she'd just thrown on, but something she'd thought about, something ordered from a catalog – a blue-striped French sailor's shirt that came down over her huge hips, and a pair of matching blue capris. Her white canvas tennis shoes were wet and dirty. I could barely see her eyes – outlined crookedly with brown eyeliner, – red and slitty from crying – from under her bangs, which were frizzy from the rain. She struck me not as a towering adversary, this crafty, scheming succubus, but a pathetic woman who had just suffered a shock.

'Oh God, is Matt here?' she started crying again, wiped her eyes with her sleeve. 'I know he said he had something at school tonight, but probably he was just lying to me, I know he lies to me all the time just to get me off his back. But is he here? If he isn't here I can go wait in the car.'

She threw her arm out behind her, her forearm rotating back at her elbow, a gesture I recognized, a Matthew gesture. It would never end.

'No, no, come in. He isn't here but he should be soon.'

I invited her in because I knew what had happened. Kiki had been right. It was something to do with Erica. Something very bad. She was in the hospital. At least. As a mother of a small child, I couldn't let in the worst thought. I left it at 'Something's happened to Erica.' I couldn't say to myself what I knew to be true: Erica was dead. I could feel my heart pounding in my head. My thighs trembled. Erica was dead. Suddenly, I was ashamed (shame still exists in modern culture, but it's the emotional equivalent of the electric typewriter; people still experience it from time to time, but it's thought to be eccentric). Poor Claudia. I had been so cruel, so hard, so uncharitable. Claudia was all alone in the world, all alone with her child and a bunch of smelly goats. And now the child was gone.

Kiki was still in the kitchen with her arm out the back door, having a cigarette.

'It's Claudia,' I yelled, as if Claudia stopped by all the time.

Claudia standing in our living room was something I thought I'd never see. It was the same as having Kevin Spacey in our living room, looking around, checking things out. 'Who reads all these books?' she asked, looking at the bookcases.

Kiki came in, her cigarette in her hand, against strict house policy. 'What's wrong? What's going on?' Even though Kiki is also a mother, she's less squeamish than I am.

Claudia's eyes welled up. She put her stubby hands in front of her face so we wouldn't see her cry, but she made so much noise that Mabel the Bad Breath Dog came downstairs from where she was sleeping to see what was going on. Mabel sniffed wildly at Claudia's legs, her ears back, tail wagging.

'She probably smells . . .' Claudia sobbed louder. '. . . Tigger's dead!'

This entire scene took place in a span of no more than five minutes. This was the longest minute of all. *Who? What's she talking about?* For a good half-second I thought she was talking about Matthew. No, he was Eeyore. Was Erica Tigger? No. Erica was Roo. I was completely confused.

'Who in the hell is Tigger?' said Kiki. 'We got your messages and thought something had happened to Erica.' I love Kiki. She is my oldest friend.

'Erica?' Claudia looked at Kiki. Her nostrils glistened with snot. She had that edge I recognized so well, that made the most innocuous question sound hostile. 'Erica is at the neighbors' playing Barbies 'n Beanies. Tigger died of coccidia, or that's what the vet said. I did all the right things. Isolated him, didn't feed him on the ground. I had him on the monensin. I got him a salt block. I did everything right. I always do everything right, and look what happens.'

Kiki and I looked at each other.

Claudia didn't stay much longer. I assured her I expected Matthew home within the half hour, but she said she had some errands and would come back. She didn't. When Matthew dragged in, exhausted from explaining to one set of parents after another why their child was getting a lower grade than they'd expected, Kiki and I filled him in, talking over each other, choking on the hilarity of it, wiping our eyes. How annoyed we'd been (well, I'd been), then how worried, then when we found out it was the *goat* . . . how hilarious was that? Well, no, no, it wasn't hilarious. It was very sad, really. Tragic, really, and after she got the salt block and everything. We screamed. We sobbed. Matthew had the same smile on his face he'd had for the parents. Kiki and I can be obnoxious. When we were living together in college we felt the true test of the worth of one of our boyfriends was whether he could endure an evening of the two of us. Only someone who loved one of us would put up with the other one, we were sure. Matthew had more than passed the test. He proved he could *live* with both of us.

'What should I do?' he asked. His voice was too plaintive.

'Matthew, why, call her back. This woman just lost her goat.'

Kiki and I screamed.

'It's nice to see you laugh,' he said.

One of the saddest things about being an ex is that you realize love doesn't conquer all. Love may conquer *a lot*, but not all. Matthew and I had the usual half-dozen exhausting discussions about why this was never going to work. Finally, one day in early spring, while I was on assignment in British Columbia, he moved out. The only things he left behind were his copies of my books, inscribed to him by me at the height of our romance.

While I'd seen Claudia in a new light the night Tigger died, it didn't make me receptive to her in the way I'd thought it would. I realized that if I stayed with Matthew it would be a lifetime of this. That if I married Matthew, I would also be marrying Claudia. And I'm not that much of an animal lover.

12

Living in High Society

I've yet to meet an ex-spouse who hasn't rediscovered the joy of watching movies. When you're first in love with your future spouse, there are lots of nights spent renting movies and snuggling beneath the afghan, juggling a bowl of popcorn on your knees. It's one of those activities that makes nesting seem romantic. You're at home, but the lights are low, and there's a movie that had a theatrical release involved. After the kids come, the TV is recast from romantic electronic hearth to full-time baby-sitter, and they're the ones watching a video. Then, the divorce, and suddenly the kids are at your ex's and the evening stretches out like a desert highway and there are four hours to kill between 7:00 and 11:00. This is how people get hooked on *Wheel of Fortune* (how else to explain its eight-thousand-year run?).

An ex's rekindled love affair with the VCR, and with

television in general (I was touched for some reason to learn that my own ex – who was anti-TV when we were married – has become a devotee of *Friends*. Our daughter reports that it's his favorite show.), provides one of the truly comforting aspects of being an ex-spouse in contemporary culture: the feeling that you are not alone. There are imaginary people on both the big and the little screen whose lives are as messed up as your own. And not just messed up, but messed up with style, an important distinction. 'Contemporary' is defined as no earlier than 1980, when Reagan (our first presidential ex) was in the White House and sitcoms like *Designing Women* proved you could be divorced and still get the best lines.

It's been said that the movies have nothing good to teach us about relationships. There was an article in the paper about it just this morning. 'Everything you learned about love at the movies – everything – is worth *bupkis*.' The article cited romantic premises that are common to the movies but never prove to be true in real life, such as, 'People Who Hate Each Other on Sight Usually End Up Falling in Love' and 'Break-Ups Are Inevitable but Can Usually Be Resolved by Chasing the Other Person Down the Street or Embarrassing Them at Work.'

The reverse is also true. Hollywood has a lot of beneficial things to teach us about not being in love. Beginning with mastering the art of the one-liner. If there's one thing all exes need to learn to do better, it's toss out a good zinger and slam the door. Not window-shattering slamming, but slamming as a nice clean punctuation mark. Imagine how much *Sturm Und Drang* would be saved if exes communicated in sparkling ripostes followed by a haughty exit.

The true dialogue between exes would never be allowed on TV, even C-Span or whatever channel it is that likes to feature Senate filibusters as part of their prime-time programming, since it would go something like this:

Ex-wife: I'm sick and tired of you showing up late to pick up the kids. Did you hear me? Sick and tired. Are you listening to me? Do you hear a word I say? Ever? Do you wonder why I couldn't stay married to you? You don't even look at me. You're doing that darting eye thing, Larry. Don't think I don't know what that means. You're just waiting to make your escape. Will you please look at me while I'm talking to you? It doesn't hurt me, you know, when you're late to pick up the kids. It hurts them. Yes, them, your own flesh and blood. They're waiting, they're sitting here waiting. Don't think they can't tell you're an hour late. You probably don't even know that Jordy's been telling time for a year and a half. Are you listening to me?

Ex-husband: mumble, mumble, mumble.

Exes have lousy reputations. We are thought to be neurotic, flighty, unable to keep our promises. We're said to be emotional slackers who prefer the easy way out. It's instructional that no one who's been through a divorce, who is an ex, now and forever, ever assumes she took the easy way out. She may wish she had worked harder to keep the marriage together, but she doesn't think that what she did was by any means easier.

'Easy would have been to stay and live separate lives. He could cheat and be emotionally absent, I could cheat and be emotionally absent, and it would have been a whole lot easier than splitting up. These days no one thinks anything of wives traveling alone, or husbands spending long nights at the office. We could have lived as roommates, and no one would presume I'd failed,' says a woman I know.

Which begs the question: What constitutes a failed marriage? It seems the only way we measure success in marriage is longevity. Woody Allen said that 98 per cent of success in life is simply showing up, and people think the same is true of marriage.

Maybe the 'death do you part' section is the only aspect of the vows that counts because it's the only part of a marriage that can be clearly measured, and thus clearly judged. The fact that you're also agreeing to love, honor, and cherish your spouse is apparently irrelevant; as long as you despise, disrespect, and ignore your husband or wife under the same roof, your marriage is considered by the world to have succeeded. The ex who claims he had a great marriage while it lasted sounds suspiciously stuck in some counterculture philosophical rut, a place where people still burn a lot of incense.

Sociologists and historians have blamed our modern urge to divorce in part on the social changes of the 1960s – the sexual revolution, the women's movement, and the advent of the Pill. The irony is that some of the behaviors that aided in the progress of the first two: learning to express your needs and desires, asserting yourself and speaking up for your rights, getting things off your chest and venting (all of which can be filed under the general heading of 'shooting your mouth off') will not help you when you're divorced.

Shooting your mouth off is a luxury in a second or third marriage. Unlike your first marriage, when it was just the two of you, the population is now large and prickly. Conflict and misunderstanding have become a way of life. Now, failing to know when to shut up is a genuine liability.

As Carol Tavris points out in *Anger: The Misunderstood Emotion*, all the complaining we do about the various exes in our lives, whether they be our exes, our ex's new spouse, or our ex-wife-in-law, does nothing to get it off our chest, but merely serves to rehearse and inflate our misery, thereby increasing the rage we'd hoped to work out by talking about it. Tavris, a social psychologist, who is also the author of *The Mismeasure of Women*, who has more than sixty pages of Notes, Index, Bibliography, and Further Reading at the back of her book, who consulted the research of dozens of psychologists and social scientists and interviewed hundreds of people for her book, in the end comes down on the side of Thomas Jefferson: 'When angry, count ten before you speak; if very angry, a hundred.' If you are an ex, make it a thousand.

The best policies in dealing with all the exes are corny, retro bits that have been put forth by either June Cleaver or Queen Elizabeth. 'If you can't say anything nice, don't say anything at all' and 'The least said, the sooner mended' are two chestnuts that come to mind. They are unthinkably unhip, and they also work.

Another bit of hopelessly out-of-date wisdom belongs to my mother, who acknowledged that sometimes things in life were just plain lousy, and there was nothing for it but to wait it out. Thus, her not-very-clever, mercilessly homespun advice:

1) Keep busy.
2) It'll pass.

Which leads me to my only conclusion about how to live as an ex, and with an ex, and not wind up in a rubber room.

Long before divorce was so common, people were stuck in the families they were born into, and the families they married into. Families were generally bigger, and not everyone got along. There were factions, intrigues, betrayals, decades-long feuds, scandals.

In the past, everyone knew what to do with family. It was a given that every family had its share of detestable members. There was lecherous Uncle Bob who liked to yammer on about various conspiracy theories, or Aunt Ruth, the passive-aggressive hypochondriac who smelled like mildew. They phoned once in a while, showed up for dinner on occasion, were entertained on holidays. You were linked with them. You were forced to find a way to deal with them, whether it meant avoiding them, ignoring them, or humoring them. The fact they were family didn't mean that you had to like them; it simply meant that you could hate them all you wanted to, but they weren't going anywhere.

Nowadays when we talk about the blended family what we tend to mean are parents and the children and stepchildren from their various marriages. We generally mean the nuclear blended family, plus the biological family members of the parent with custody.

But the distressing fact is this: Your ex or your ex-wife-in-law or your ex-husband-in-law is as much a part of the blended family as the unendurable Uncle Bob. This is nothing but bad news, I know. This ex, this person who's become your personal plague of locusts – I don't care what your relationship once *was*, now it's so unpleasant you would exchange the whole never-ending predicament for a tax audit in a heartbeat – is now and forever part of the gang. Never forget: Marriage, with children, really is forever. One way or another.

There is, however, a bona fide reason for being civil and considerate to an ex you might normally despise: a child who loves him. Tolerating an ex for the sake of a child is a far better reason for putting up with someone you detest than the fact that he's your mother's uncle by marriage.

I wrote a magazine article about extreme women athletes, women who engage in the so-called extreme sports of sky surfing (in which they do things like jump out of an airplane with a board strapped to their feet to surf the air currents as they freefall) and extreme skiing, where they descend Alpine couloirs so steep that a simple fall means death. They hang glide, rock climb, surf waves so big that a wipeout spells certain drowning. I interviewed at least a dozen of these remarkable women, and not one of them has a family. When I asked a woman who'd spent her life kayaking down rapids so steep that they would qualify as waterfalls in anyone else's mind why she had never married or had children, she laughed, 'Are you kidding? Now, that's terrifying.'

Instead of calling it the 'blended family' – which sounds culinary and flimsy – we should call it the 'extreme family'. This emphasizes the degree of brute tolerance required for the task of integrating you and your ex or exes, your new partner's ex or exes, your parents and siblings, your ex or exes' parents and siblings, his ex or exes's parents and siblings, the children from your first marriage or first and second marriages, the children from his first marriage or first and second marriages, miscellaneous pets.

And don't forget the ex-sofa.

A little over a year after Matthew and I broke up I bought a house not far from Lucinda, the cheerful ex with the frat-house decor who subscribed to a policy of nonattachment. It has maple wood floors, built-in bookcases and sideboard, a sunroom shaded in the summer by an old fig tree, a pair of raccoons living under the porch, and the kind of water pressure that won't allow you to run the dishwasher and flush the toilet on the same day.

A bit later, in a move that caused even the gimlet-eyed women of the Mae West Dinner Party – two of whom, it should be noted, had recently reentered the institution of marriage – to swoon, I lived out the secret fantasy of millions of female office workers the world over: I married my UPS man.

Dan is divorced, not divarried. His ex-wife lives fifteen hundred miles away, and he hasn't laid eyes on her since

1995. He has full custody of his daughter, Tess, whom he raised alone from infancy. Like Matthew, Dan has ocean eyes with whites that turn pink when he's distressed. He has a dimple in his chin, and long legs that sit in his hip sockets in a most exciting manner. He is also the founder and lone member of the Heterosexual Man's Musical Comedy Appreciation Society. His all-time favorite is *South Pacific,* although *Singing in the Rain* rates a close second.

After Dan proposed (on one knee, just like in the olden days!) I e-mailed Spud for a consult. Spud had been married twice, and had taken a dim view of the whole Matthew business. I was surprised to receive this:

<<Karbs, way to score. Does he drive one of those big-ass trucks? No power steering in those suckers. Do I think you're insane for getting remarried? Not at all. Nobody ever says to a surgeon, 'You've already done that knee operation. Why would you want to do it again?' And conversely, would you want to be the surgeon's first patient? Don't think so. The only people who should be allowed to get married are people who've been divorced, since they're the only ones who know the degree to which they could be completely screwing up their lives. Why we think a pair of horny 22-year-olds are better candidates for marriage than a jaded old crone like you, I'll never know. And here's

something else. Fuck love. I pay $700 a month for health insurance for me and the kids. Your guy's a *Teamster*. His benefits are the best in the free world.>>

One night Dan insisted we rent *High Society*, the 1956 musical remake of *The Philadelphia Story*. He argued that despite the fact *The Philadelphia Story* won all those Oscar nominations, and had Cary Grant and Jimmy Stewart, who, he conceded, were better in their roles as C.K. Dexter Haven and Mike Connor than were Bing Crosby and Frank Sinatra, *High Society* was a better movie.

We cuddled beneath a quilt, the bowl of popcorn balanced on our knees. Tess and Katherine were upstairs, playing horses. We could hear the little plastic hooves scraping on the wood floor.

Dan said, 'It has Cole Porter and Grace Kelly. You can't beat that.'

I said, 'It also has a big mitigating factor, fruity Bing Crosby, whose appeal was definitely generational. He's too Lawrence Welk, too ba-ba-ba-boo. And that scene where he and Grace Kelly are sailing on *The True Love* and she has her head in his lap and he's wearing that captain's hat and playing the *accordian*. And let's talk about the age thing. He's like twenty years older than she is. Isn't part of the reason we're supposed to believe she goes back to him at the end is that they grew up together?'

'That was only in *The Philadelphia Story*. In *High Society* he's a musician.'

'And that scene with Louis Armstrong. Bing Crosby and hot jazz. That's like Pat Boone and heavy metal.'

'All right. Point granted. Kelly would never pass up Sinatra for Crosby.'

'Never. There's that hot scene by the pool where Sinatra sings "You're Sensational" to her. It's too hot. No woman would pass up that for an old guy in a captain's hat.'

If *High Society* was remade today, Tracy Lord would be played by Gwyneth Paltrow, who would choose neither boring George, her fiancé, nor even C.K. Dexter Haven, her ex-husband, but the writer, Mike Connor, the new man, the one who wooed her best. It may or may not be the right decision, but then Tracy Lord would be like the rest of the generation. She would be a woman with a first marriage, a broken engagement, and a second marriage under her belt, all by age twenty-eight.

To manage this with style, Tracy would have heeded her mother's wisdom. In a classic screwball comedy scene, everyone suddenly finds him- or herself out on the terrace at the same time: Mother Lord; Uncle Willy; Tracy's little sister, Caroline; the reporters from *Spy* magazine, including Mike Connor, who is already smitten with Tracy; Tracy herself; and George, Tracy's dull fiancé. Who should choose to pop over but Tracy's ex, C.K. Dexter Haven.

It's a great, awkward moment. To make every one feel at ease, Mother Lord says: 'We're all very friendly! It's the only civilized way to behave!'

Bibliography

No writer works in a vacuum. More often than not her greatest companions and supporters during the long journey of composition and revision are fellow travelers who've written about similar subjects, however tangentially. I am indebted to the authors of the following works.

Ackerman, Diane; *A Natural History of Love*, Vintage Books

Ahrons, Constance R., Ph.D.; *The Good Divorce: Keeping Your Family Together When Your Marriage Comes Apart*, HarperCollins

Applewhite, Ashton; *Cutting Loose: Why Women Who End Their Marriages Do So Well*, HarperCollins

Bloom, Claire; *Leaving a Doll's House: A Memoir*, Little, Brown and Company

Ferris, Blake (editor); *The Ex-Files: New Stories About Old Flames*, Context Books

Fisher, Helen, Ph.D.; *Anatomy of Love: A Natural History of Mating, Marriage, and Why We Stray*, Fawcett Columbine

Euripides, *Medea*; Dover Publications

Feiffer, George; *Divorce: An Oral Portrait*, The New Press

Harris, Janice Hubbard; *Edwardian Stories of Divorce*, Rutgers University Press

Huffington, Arianna Stassinopoulos; *Picasso: Creator and Destroyer*, Simon and Schuster

Kaganoff, Penny and Spano, Susan (editors); *Men on Divorce: The Other Side of the Story*, Harcourt, Brace

Kaganoff, Penny and Spano, Susan (editors); *Women on Divorce: A Bedside Companion*, Harcourt Brace

Kline, Kris and Pew, Stephen, Ph.D.; *For the Sake of the Children: How to Share your Children with your Ex-Spouse in Spite of Your Anger*, Prima Publishing

Kramer, Peter D.; *Should You Leave? A Psychiatrist Explores Intimacy and Autonomy – and the Nature of Advice*, Scribner

Lindsey, Karen; *Divorced, Beheaded, Survived: A Feminist Reinterpretation of the Wives of Henry VIII*, Addison Wesley

Madanes, Cloe and Madanes, Claudio; *The Secret Meaning of Money: How It Binds Together Families in Love, Envy, Compassion, or Anger*, Jossey-Bass Publishers

Mailer, Adele; *The Last Party: Scenes from My Life with Norman Mailer*, Barricade Books

O'Brian, Patrick; *Picasso: A Biography*, W.W. Norton

Riley, Glenda; *Divorce: An American Tradition*, University of Nebraska Press

Shimberg, Elaine Fantle; *Blending Families: A Guide for Parents, Step-Parents, Grandparents and Everyone Building a Successful New Family*, Berkley Books

Shoshanna, Brenda, Ph.D.; *Why Men Leave*, Penguin Putnam

Tavris, Carol; *Anger: The Misunderstood Emotion*, Touchstone Books

Taylor, John; *Falling: The Story of One Marriage*, Random House

BIBLIOGRAPHY

Trafford, Abigail, *Crazy Time: Surviving Divorce and Rebuilding a New Life*, HarperPerennial

Thurman, Judith; *Secrets of the Flesh: A Life of Colette*, Ballantine

Weir, Alison; *The Six Wives of Henry VIII*, Ballantine Books

Wallerstein, Judith S. and Blakeslee, Sandra; *Second Chances: Men, Women and Children a Decade After Divorce*, Houghton Mifflin

Whitehead, Barbara DeFoe; *The Divorce Culture*, Knopf

Wymard, Ellie, Ph.D.; *Men on Divorce: Conversations with Ex-Husbands*, Hay House

A NOTE ON THE AUTHOR

Karen Karbo is the author of three novels, *Motherhood Made a Man Out of Me*, *The Diamond Lane*, and *Trespassers Welcome Here*. Her nonfiction has appeared in *Vogue*, *Esquire*, *Entertainment Weekly*, *The New Republic*, and *The New York Times*. She grew up in Southern California and now lives in Portland, Oregon, with her family.